THE ROMANS

Anthony Marks
Graham Tingay

Illustrated by **Ian Jackson**
and **Gerald Wood**

Designed by **Radhi Parekh, Robert Walster**
and **Iain Ashman**

History consultant: **Anne Millard**

Edited by **Jane Chisholm**

Map illustrations by **Robert Walster**

Further illustrations by **Peter Dennis, Richard Draper, James Field** and **Nigel Wright**

With thanks to **Lynn Bresler**

Contents

About this book

The city of Rome was founded in about 753BC. By 100BC the Romans had a huge empire centred round the Mediterranean Sea. It lasted for centuries, and its influence has continued to the present day. This book describes both the rise and decline of Rome as a world power and the way people lived from day to day.

Dates

Many dates in this book are from the period before the birth of Christ. They are shown by the letters BC which stand for 'Before Christ'. (Dates in this period are counted backwards from Christ's birth; for example, the period from 100BC to 199BC is called the second century BC.)

Dates in the period after the Christ's birth are indicated by the letters AD, which stand for *Anno Domini* ('Year of our Lord'). To avoid confusion AD and BC have been used throughout the book.

Some dates begin with the abbreviation 'c.'. This stands for *circa*, the Latin for 'about', and is used when historians are unsure exactly when an event took place.

Periods of Roman history

Experts divide Roman history into two main periods. The first is known as the republic, which probably began in began in 510 or 509BC. It is followed by the Empire, which began in 27BC when the first Roman emperor took power. Throughout this book the word Empire has been given a capital letter only when it is used to mean 'the period of rule by emperors' rather than simply 'Roman territory'.

How we know about the Romans

Although Roman civilization began more than two thousand years ago, we have plenty of information about how the Romans lived. Much of it comes from the sources listed below, and has been used as the basis for this book.

Many Roman buildings survive almost intact. They tell us about building technology and styles of architecture. Ruined towns, roads and aqueducts provide information about civil engineering and planning. Buildings and ruins often contain sculptures, wall-paintings and mosaics†, many of which include scenes of daily life.

The Pantheon in Rome remains almost as the Romans built it.

Shoes like this were found near the River Thames in London.

Buildings contain objects that the Romans used, including tools, utensils, ornaments and toys. Some are well preserved, especially at sites where there were volcanic eruptions, because ash and mud have protected them from decay.

Fragments of pottery help us to determine the dates of Roman remains, as different styles of pot are easy to identify and date. If, for example, experts can recognize and date pieces of pottery at the bottom of a well, they can give a rough date to other objects found in the same place.

Archaeologists store and record each item they find.

Many Roman coins are easy to date, as they depict events that are mentioned in Roman books. If found at archaeological sites, they can indicate when buildings were erected or were in use. In addition, coins found in such places as India and Scandinavia suggest that Roman traders travelled far beyond the limits of Roman territory.

This coin commemorates the Roman occupation of Egypt.

Much of our information about the Romans comes from their own writings. Very few Roman books or manuscripts themselves have survived to modern times, but we have copies of them which were made mostly by monks in the middle ages and by later scholars. They include works by many Roman writers about history, politics and philosophy, as well as plays, poems and letters. These give us insight into the lives and characters of Roman people.

Other written evidence survives in the form of stone inscriptions. Details of laws, legal contracts, financial transactions and military records were carved into the walls of public buildings all over the Roman world. In addition, graves and tombs give us details, both written and pictorial, of the lives and deaths of their occupants.

This carving on a stone tomb shows a Roman shipbuilder at work.

Key dates

On some pages of this book there are charts that summarize the events of the particular period. There is also a large chart on pages 88-89 that lists all the events in the book.

Unfamiliar words

Words are written in *italic* type to indicate that they are Latin (the language of the Romans). Words followed by a dagger symbol, such as citizen†, are explained in the glossary that begins on page 81. If a person's name is followed by this symbol, you can read more about them in the 'Who's who' on pages 84-87.

Places

There are small maps on many pages to show where certain events took place. Some of these are based on a projection that may be unfamiliar. This has been used to enable large areas of Europe to be shown in a compact space.

Reference

At the back of the book there is an appendix. It contains a glossary, biographies of important Romans, a detailed date chart and other information. It is followed by an index.

The founding of Rome

The city of Rome was founded in the 8th century BC, in the country now called Italy. The history of the area has been affected by its geography. Most of Italy is rough, hilly country which rises to a central mountain range called the Apennines.

Some of the most fertile agricultural land is near the west coast, on three small plains around the rivers Arno, Volturno and Tiber. Rome was established on the plain of Latium, around the River Tiber.

Early migration into Italy

Long before Rome was founded, several groups of people migrated into Italy from other parts of Europe. This map shows the routes of these people.

From around 2000BC, migrants from central Europe (including a group now known as the Latins) drifted over the Alps into Italy. They settled mainly in the north-west.

The Alps

River Po

River Arno

ETRURIA

River Tiber

The Apennines

Rome

Alba Longa

Laurentum

LATIUM

River Volturno

Naples

MAGNA GRAECIA

Greek vase

Around 750BC, Greek migrants began to settle in southern Italy and on the coast of Sicily. Their influence became so strong in this area that the Romans later called it *Magna Graecia* (Great Greece).

SICILY

Syracuse

GREECE

- → Route of migrants from central Europe
- → Route of migrants from Greece
- → Possible route of Etruscans
- → Route of migrants from North Africa

Phoenician pot

Some migrants, including a group called the Phoenicians†, came from North Africa to Sicily, Sardinia and Corsica.

Etruscan mask

People known as the Etruscans (see below) are thought to have reached Italy by sea about 800BC. They settled in two main groups to the north and south of the plain of Latium.

The Etruscans

Little is known about the origins of the Etruscans. They may have come from Asia Minor (now Turkey) before settling in the part of Italy known as Etruria. Their civilization, based on a group of well-planned, fortified cities ruled by kings, flourished between about 800BC and 400BC. The Etruscans adopted the Greek alphabet, and were skilled workers in bronze, iron and precious metals. They traded widely with Greece and the Middle East, and became extremely powerful and influential (see opposite). At their peak they controlled an area from the River Po to Naples.

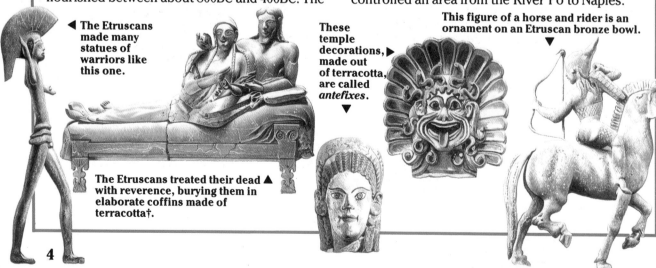

◄ The Etruscans made many statues of warriors like this one.

These temple decorations, ► made out of terracotta, are called *antefixes*. ▼

This figure of a horse and rider is an ornament on an Etruscan bronze bowl. ▼

The Etruscans treated their dead ▲ with reverence, burying them in elaborate coffins made of terracotta†.

The first settlements

Rome grew from a cluster of villages founded by Latin immigrants about 25km (6 miles) inland on the River Tiber. There was an island there, and a ford where the river could be crossed. This was the furthest point that could be reached by ship before the water became too shallow.

The villages were built on a group of seven hills; one of the first to be occupied was known as the Palatine Hill. They were in a good position for trade, because they were on the most important routes for travelling merchants. As they grew richer, the settlements merged into one town.

An early Roman settlement

Little is known about Rome's early history, so we must rely mainly on legend. The date traditionally given for the founding of the city is 753BC. The actual date is uncertain, but it is likely that the villages merged around this time. According to one legend, the Greeks laid siege to the city of Troy (near the coast of modern Turkey) and killed nearly all the occupants. One Trojan prince, Aeneas, escaped by sea and sailed to Italy.

Aeneas sailing from Troy

Aeneas landed at Laurentum on the west coast of Italy. He formed an alliance with Latinus, the king of the Latins, and married his daughter Lavinia. Aeneas's son Ascanius founded a city called Alba Longa (see map opposite). He was the first of a long line of kings who ruled for about 400 years. When the last king was overthrown, his twin grandsons Romulus and Remus were left to die by the River Tiber. A wolf found them and looked after them.

This statue shows the twins being suckled by the wolf.

A new city

When the twins grew up they decided to set up a new city on the spot where they had been left to drown. They held a sacred ceremony to mark the boundary with a plough, but Remus jumped over the furrow in mockery. Romulus was enraged and killed his brother, gave his own name to the city and became its first ruler. Romulus was followed by six kings: Numa Pompilius, Tullus Hostilius, Ancus Martius, Tarquinius Priscus, Servius Tullius, and Tarquinius Superbus. Parts of a wall around Rome, known as the Servian Wall (see map) and once thought to have been built by Servius Tullius, still remain.

Servian Wall
Quirinal Hill
Viminal Hill
River Tiber
Capitoline Hill
Esquiline Hill
Palatine Hill
Caelian Hill
Aventine Hill

The influence of the Etruscans

For much of this early period Rome was ruled by the Etruscans, who were more advanced than the Latins. Under their influence Rome became a large city that dominated the Tiber valley. But gradually the Etruscans lost their hold on Latium. Finally the last Etruscan king was expelled from Rome. The date traditionally given for this is 510 or 509BC. After this Rome became an independent republic (for details of how the state was governed, see pages 10-11), but the Romans inherited many things from their Etruscan rulers.

The Etruscans ▲ built Rome's first drainage system.

Romans wore a robe called the *toga* (see page 42). It was based on an Etruscan robe like the one shown on this statue. ▶

Etruscan soldiers had an official symbol called the *fasces* – an axe tied to a bundle of sticks. It was later adopted ▶ by the Romans.

Key dates

From c.2000BC Immigrants enter Italy from the North.

c.800BC Etruscans arrive in Italy by sea.

753BC Date traditionally given for the founding of Rome.

c.750BC Greek migrants settle on the southern coasts of Sicily and Italy.

510BC or 509BC Last king expelled from Rome; republic founded.

c.400BC Decline of Etruscans.

The early republic

Other cities in Latium formed an alliance and challenged the new republic† of Rome. The Romans were defeated at Lake Regillus in 496BC, and forced to join the alliance. Over the next century Rome fought many wars against mountain tribes who attacked Roman territory.

At this time, most Romans were poor farmers who had to fight wars simply to defend their land. However, by 400BC, after years of tough fighting and clever political tactics, Roman territory had doubled in size and Rome had become the dominant partner in the Latin alliance.

Fierce mountain tribes called the Volsci, Aequi and Sabini attacked Roman farms.

The Gauls attack Rome

In 387BC the Gauls, people from northern Europe, defeated the Roman army at the River Allia and invaded Rome. According to the historian Livy†, most of the population had fled in terror. Apart from some troops only the Roman senators† remained, sitting calmly in the courtyards of their houses. The Gauls stared in amazement, but when one of them touched a senator's beard, the senator struck him with his ivory staff.

A massacre followed. The Gauls murdered the senators and then began to destroy Rome. Only the Capitoline Hill survived. According to legend the Gauls attacked it at night, but disturbed some geese that were kept at a temple. The geese warned the Romans of the Gauls' approach. Finally the invaders were bribed with gold to leave the ruined city. The other Latin cities were delighted to see Rome overthrown.

The Gauls attacked Capitoline Hill by night.

Expansion in Italy

Slowly the Romans recovered from this disaster. In about 380BC they rebuilt much of Rome, and constructed a strong wall around all its seven hills. By improving their army (see page 14), they began to regain lost territory. In 338BC, with the help of the Samnites, a tribe from central Italy, the Romans defeated an alliance of Latin cities. This made them the most powerful people in Latium. This map shows the position of the tribes in Italy around 338BC.

Etruscans
Sabini
Aequi △ Lake Regillus
• Rome
Hernici
Volsci
ITALY
Samnites
LATIUM

The wars with the Samnites

In 326BC Naples, a city in southern Italy, asked Rome for help against the Samnites. The Samnites objected to Rome's growing influence in the area, and a series of wars broke out. These wars lasted 40 years until the Samnites were defeated, along with their allies the Gauls and Etruscans. During this period, Rome also won important victories against the Aequi and Hernici tribes. By fighting hard and making clever alliances, Rome began to dominate northern and central Italy.

Samnite soldiers

The Pyrrhic wars

In 282BC Thurii, a Greek town in southern Italy, asked Rome to send a force of soldiers to protect them from the Lucanians, allies of the Samnites. Rome did so, and soon other cities had also put themselves under Roman protection. The nearby Greek city of Tarentum resented this and quarrelled with a Roman delegation. Tarentum was a commercial city, unable to match Rome's army, but it had provoked a situation from which it could not retreat. So in 280BC it hired the army of King Pyrrhus of Epirus in northern Greece.

Pyrrhus advanced on the Romans with 25,000 soldiers and 20 elephants.

Statue of Pyrrhus

Pyrrhus defeated the Romans in 280BC and 279BC, but vast numbers of his own soldiers were killed. He said 'If we win one more victory against the Romans we shall be totally ruined.' This is why the phrase 'Pyrrhic victory' is sometimes used when a winner's losses are greater than his gains. Pyrrhus withdrew to Sicily, then returned to Italy in 276BC. He was decisively defeated the following year, and in 272BC Tarentum surrendered. By 264BC Rome dominated the whole of Italy and was recognized as a major power in the Mediterranean.

This plate shows a war elephant from Pyrrhus's army.

Colonization in Italy

The Romans succeeded in dominating Italy by combining military strength and political astuteness. When they conquered an area they offered it an alliance, and drew up a treaty that defined the status of the new ally. Some places, like Tusculum, had full Roman citizenship. Others, such as Spoletium, were given 'Latin rights', which included some of the advantages of citizenship†. Other areas kept domestic independence, but Rome dictated their foreign policies. All allied states had to provide troops for the Roman army.

Rome also formed colonies of Romans or Latins in strategic places throughout Italy. By building roads and improving communications the Romans united the various Italian tribes. Gradually the Latin language and the Roman way of life spread, and linguistic and cultural differences between different areas were reduced.

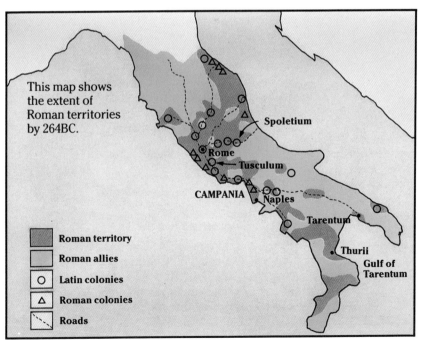

This map shows the extent of Roman territories by 264BC.

Spoletium

Rome

Tusculum

CAMPANIA

Naples

Tarentum

Thurii

Gulf of Tarentum

- Roman territory
- Roman allies
- ○ Latin colonies
- △ Roman colonies
- ⟍⟍ Roads

Key dates

510-509BC Founding of republic.

496BC Romans forced to join Latin alliance after Battle of Lake Regillus.

By 400BC Rome has emerged as the dominant partner in the Latin alliance.

387BC Gauls attack Rome.

338BC Romans and Samnites defeat other Latin cities.

326BC War breaks out between Romans and Samnites.

286BC Rome defeats Samnites, Gauls and Etruscans, and takes control of northern and central Italy.

280BC Beginning of Pyrrhic wars.

275BC Pyrrhus's army defeated at the Battle of Beneventum.

272BC Tarentum surrenders.

By 264BC Rome dominates the whole of Italy.

The expansion of Rome

While Rome was becoming powerful in Italy, the western Mediterranean was under the control of the Carthaginians. Carthage, a city on the North African coast, was founded about 814BC by the Phoenicians, a people originally from the Middle East. Carthage was the centre of a vast commercial empire. While their trading interests did not conflict, Rome and Carthage left each other in peace. But in 264BC, a series of wars began between them. These are known as the Punic wars, after the Latin word for Phoenician. This map shows western Europe at the start of the Punic wars.

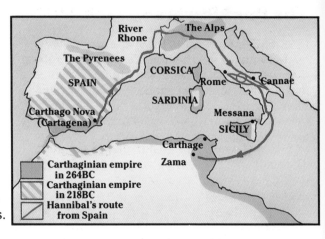

Carthaginian empire in 264BC
Carthaginian empire in 218BC
Hannibal's route from Spain

The first Punic war, 264-241BC

In 264BC Carthage occupied Messana in north-east Sicily. The Greek cities in south Italy, under Roman protection, saw this as a threat. The Romans sent an army to Sicily and war broke out. It took the Romans 20 years to expel the Carthaginians from Sicily. To do so they first had to find ways of overcoming Carthage's superior naval skills.

The Romans invented a spiked drawbridge called the *corvus*. It was dropped onto the enemy's ship, enabling Roman soldiers to charge aboard.

The Romans had no experience of sea warfare, but they twice built huge fleets (see page 20) and won victories, then lost all their ships in violent storms. The Carthaginians were eventually defeated by a third fleet in 241BC. Under the terms of the peace, Rome acquired Sicily (its first overseas territory). In addition, over the next ten years, Carthage had to pay the Romans a huge sum of money (known as an indemnity) as compensation for the cost of the war.

The Romans took Sardinia from Carthage in 238BC, and later seized Corsica too. They probably took this aggressive action to deprive Carthage of its island bases in the Mediterranean.

The second Punic war, 218-201BC

In search of a new empire, the Carthaginians invaded and conquered Spain between 237BC and 219BC. Hannibal, the Carthaginian general in Spain and a lifelong enemy of Rome, provoked the second Punic war. He launched a surprise attack on the Romans by marching over the Pyrenees in 218BC with 35,000 men and 37 elephants. He ferried the elephants over the River Rhone on rafts, then forced his way into Italy over the Alps.

The Romans were completely overwhelmed. Hannibal was a great general, and his troops won battle after battle. At Cannae in 216BC they destroyed an entire Roman army. Hannibal fought in Italy for 16 years and suffered no major defeats. However, he never conquered Rome itself, and the Romans remained defiant. After Cannae they waited until the next generation became old enough to form a new army.

Unable to defeat Hannibal in Italy, the Romans invaded and conquered Spain, then attacked

Crossing the Alps in winter, Hannibal lost nearly 10,000 men and all but one of the elephants. But he still had the advantage of being able to surprise the Romans.

Carthage. Hannibal was recalled to Africa and defeated at Zama in 202BC. Rome seized the Carthaginian territories in Spain. In the following decades the Romans conquered much of south-west Europe and became the major power in the western Mediterranean.

The third Punic war (149-146BC)

The third Punic war (149-146BC) ended with the destruction of Carthage itself. The territory became the Roman province† of Africa.

The destruction of Carthage

The Roman conquest of Europe

Gradually the Romans were also drawn into wars to the east of Italy. Some small states asked them for protection, and larger ones pursued aggressive policies that provoked Roman retaliation. Success in a series of wars against Macedonia (215-168BC), and in other conflicts further south, increased the Romans' military presence in Greece. In 146BC they crushed an uprising in Corinth and destroyed the city, as a warning to others not to undermine their authority. The rest of Greece was put under a Roman governor. Soon the entire Mediterranean came under Roman control.

By 49BC Julius Caesar† had extended the province† of Gaul to the River Rhine and the English Channel.

Gallia Narbonensis (southern Gaul; modern Provence) was added to Roman territories in 121BC.

This map shows Roman conquests around the Mediterranean by about 14BC.

English Channel

Hostile tribes were crushed in Spain and on both sides of the Alps.

River Rhine

Cisalpine Gaul became part of Italy in 42BC.

In 133BC Pergamum was bequeathed to Rome by its king. It became the Roman province of Asia.

Bithynia, Pontus, Syria and Crete were annexed between 75 and 64BC.

GAUL

BITHYNIA

Rome seized Carthaginian territory in 202BC, then slowly moved northwards in Spain.

MACEDONIA

PONTUS

ASIA

Mediterranean Sea

ACHAEA

Corinth

SYRIA

NUMIDIA

In 146BC Carthage became the Roman province of Africa.

CRETE

Cilicia became a Roman province in 102BC.

Boundary of Roman territory

Cyrene was bequeathed to Rome in 96BC by King Ptolemy Apion. It became the Roman province of Cyrenaica.

AFRICA

CYRENAICA

In 31BC Octavian† took over Egypt.

EGYPT

Key dates

264-241BC First Punic war.

238BC Romans seize Sardinia. War breaks out again.

218-201BC Second Punic war.

216BC Roman army destroyed at Cannae.

202BC Hannibal recalled to Carthage and defeated at Zama.

149-146BC Third Punic war. Carthage destroyed.

146BC Romans destroy Corinth as a warning to other cities. Start of Roman rule in Greece.

133BC-31BC Major expansion of Roman territories in Mediterranean.

31BC Octavian takes over Egypt.

Rome's social and political structure

The occupants of Roman territory fell into two groups: *cives* (Roman citizens) and *peregrini* (foreigners). Citizens had special privileges. They were allowed to vote in elections and to serve in the army; non-citizens were not. At first only people with Roman parents qualified for citizenship. Later the government began granting citizenship to certain foreigners. These two groups were further divided, as shown below. There were three classes of citizen. These divisions began very early in Rome's history. The non-citizens included provincials (people who lived outside Rome itself but within Roman territory; see pages 26-27), and slaves (see page 53).

Citizens

The richest citizens, called patricians, were probably descended from early rich landowners and political leaders.

Equites (businessmen) were descendants of the first Roman cavalry officers (see page 14).

Plebeians (commoners) were probably the descendants of poor farmers and traders.

Non-citizens

Slaves were owned by other people. They had no freedom or rights. During the early republic there were very few slaves, but later the number grew.

Provincials did not have the full rights of Romans. They also had to pay taxes to the government in Rome. Citizens did not pay these taxes.

Families

The concept of the family was very important to the Romans. Every family was led by a *paterfamilias* (father), and included his wife and children, his sons' wives and children, and all their property and slaves. When the *paterfamilias* died, each of his sons might become the head of a new family, linked by name to the old one. The resulting chain of related families formed a clan called a *gens*.

The *paterfamilias* commanded awe and respect. He held the power of life and death over the family, and looked after the welfare of its members. He also directed the family's religious activities (see page 62).

The patronage system

The client visited his patron regularly to be given food or money.

People who did not have the legal protection of a family (for example, newcomers to Rome, ex-slaves, or people who had left their own families) could attach themselves to an existing family. They were known as *clientes* (clients), and their protectors as *patroni* (patrons). The *cliens* gave his *patronus* political and social support in return for financial and legal protection.

The government of the Roman republic

Rome was governed by the Senate, originally a group of 100 men who were leaders of important patrician families. Later the number of senators was increased; by 82BC there were 600. Senators normally served for life. Each year citizens voted in an election, known as an Assembly, to select senators to be government officials. The various officials and their duties are shown below.

Two consuls (the most senior officials) were elected each year. They managed the affairs of the Senate and the Roman armies. After their year in office, consuls could become proconsuls (governors in the provinces†).

Eight *praetores* were elected, mainly to be judges in the law courts (see pages 74-75).

Four *aediles* looked after markets, streets and public buildings. They also organized and paid for public games (see pages 58-59), and could become very popular.

Each year 20 financial administrators called *quaestores* were chosen. They did not have to be senators to be elected. After 80BC anyone elected as a *quaestor* also became a senator.

Every five years two *censores* were chosen from the former consuls. *Censores* served for 18 months. They revised the membership of the Senate, removed unworthy members, and enrolled new senators. They were also responsible for making the state's contracts for public works and tax collection.

In emergencies the state could nominate a dictator, who normally ruled for a maximum of six months. He had absolute authority over everyone else. A dictator could nominate his own assistant, called the *magister equitum* (master of the horse).

Social change

At first only patricians could become senators, and they tried to preserve their privileged positions. But many plebeians lived in poverty, and their resentment of the patricians' power caused violent political struggles. The plebeians went on strike five times, threatening to leave Rome whenever they were most needed as soldiers. In 494BC, after the first strike, they set up their own Popular Assembly, which excluded patricians. Each year they chose officials called tribunes to protect their interests.

The plebeians held frequent demonstrations on the streets of Rome.

To pacify the plebeians, the patricians gave them the power to stop any laws passed by the Senate. The plebeians then demanded that the laws be written down and published, to stop judges using unwritten laws against them. A list of laws, known as the Twelve Tables, was published in 450BC.

The plebeians slowly won the right to stand for official positions. The first plebeian consul was elected in 366BC. In 287BC a ruling was passed stating that all resolutions passed by the Popular Assembly should become law. But during the Carthaginian wars (see pages 8-9), plebeian generals misused their power. Many people thought that only the patricians had the ability to run the country during a war. So the patricians still kept political control.

11

The end of the Roman republic

The expansion of Roman territories abroad led to problems in Rome itself, and placed a strain on the government. There were constant struggles for power between the Senate, the *equites*† and the plebeians†. A period of dictatorships and civil wars finally caused the downfall of the republic†.

During the wars with Carthage, many small farms were ruined by neglect or military devastation. After the wars few farmers could afford to repair the damage. Gradually their land, and much public land as well, was taken over by rich landowners who created new, large farms.

The large farms were worked cheaply and efficiently by slaves, often captives taken in the wars.

Most of the people who had lost their land flocked to the cities, where they remained unemployed. Many others lived in poverty in rural areas. As a result, Rome was left short of soldiers, as only property owners could serve in the army.

Unemployed plebeians

In 133BC a tribune†, Tiberius Gracchus, proposed that public land that had been illegally seized by rich landowners should be given to the landless poor. The Popular Assembly† passed a law, and a committee was set up to redistribute the land. But the Senate disagreed, because many senators were landowners who wanted to keep their farms. Tiberius was killed in a riot that was provoked by the Senate. In 123BC his brother Gaius was elected tribune. Before he too was murdered, he passed radical laws that challenged the Senate's power.

The rise of dictators

For the next 60 or 70 years there was constant political unrest. Some senators, called *optimates*, wanted to maintain the Senate's firm control. Others, called *populares*, were keen to spread the control more widely. They asked the tribunes, *equites* and plebeians for support, but often only because they wanted more personal power.

In 107BC Marius, a military commander, was elected consul†. He was given command of an army fighting in Africa and soon won the war. He was made consul each year from 105BC to 100BC, breaking the rule that consuls had to be replaced annually. The reason given was that he was needed to prevent tribes invading Italy from Gaul.

This coin, showing Marius in a chariot, was issued to celebrate a military victory.

Marius succeeded in his task, but to do so he had to reorganize the army (see page 15). He improved weapons and training, and allowed all citizens† to become soldiers whether or not they owned land. Thousands of unemployed men volunteered. However, the state made no provision for soldiers without property. This meant that when they retired they depended on their generals to obtain money or land for them from the Senate. They were therefore more loyal to the individual generals than to the state.

Marius and his troops

Coin showing head of Sulla

In 88BC Sulla, Marius's former lieutenant, became consul and took command of the army against Mithridates, the king of Asia Minor. When a tribune passed a resolution giving command to Marius, Sulla led his army on Rome. He took control of the city and drove Marius into exile.

As soon as Sulla had been called away from Rome once more, Marius raised an army and took control of the city. After executing hundreds of his political rivals he died in 86BC. Sulla returned in 84BC, destroyed his enemies, and ruled as dictator from 82 to 80BC. He gave supreme power back to the Senate, depriving *equites* and tribunes of most of their influence. He then retired, and died in 78BC.

However, Sulla's arrangements were quickly undermined by a general called Pompey. He won victories in Spain in 71BC, and helped the senator Crassus to crush a slave rebellion led by a slave called Spartacus. In 70BC, Pompey and Crassus demanded to be made consuls, threatening to use military force if they were refused. Once in office they swept away Sulla's legislation, and gave power back to the tribunes.

Bust of Pompey

Pompey and Caesar

In 60BC Pompey, Crassus and a rising politician, Julius Caesar, formed an alliance. Caesar became consul in 59BC. After his year in office he served as a proconsul† in Gaul for ten years. He extended Roman territory throughout Spain and Gaul, and

Bust of Caesar

invaded Britain in 55BC. A brilliant general, he became very popular with the army and the people.

In 53BC Crassus died in battle, and a year later the Senate House was burned down in a riot. To restore order, the Senate persuaded Pompey to become consul by himself. Fearing that Caesar would return to Rome and take their power away, the *optimates* turned Caesar and Pompey against each other. They forced Caesar into civil war, relying on Pompey to win. Caesar led his army on Rome in 49BC, and seized power. He defeated the armies of Pompey and the Senate in Spain (49BC and 45BC), Greece (48BC) and Africa (46BC).

Caesar arriving in Rome

Caesar's rule

Once in power, Caesar passed laws to relieve hardship, reduce debts and improve the administration. His rule brought a brief period of political stability, during which he also began many building projects in Rome and elsewhere.

Caesar was a great public speaker and an extremely popular leader.

Caesar was made dictator for life, and became the most powerful ruler Rome had ever known. Although his reforms were popular, he acted as if he were king, taking decisions without consulting the Senate. This worried many people, who believed his power threatened the republic. On 15th March 44BC Caesar was murdered by a group of conspirators led by the senators Brutus and Cassius. They hoped to restore the republic, but they failed. Caesar's heir, Octavian (see page 22) created a military dictatorship which lasted another 500 years.

The murder of Caesar

Key dates

133BC Land reforms of Tiberius Gracchus.
123BC Gaius Gracchus elected tribune.
107BC Marius first elected consul.
88BC Sulla becomes consul, then marches on Rome.
86BC Marius dies.
82-80BC Sulla rules Rome as dictator.
78BC Sulla dies.
70BC Pompey and Crassus elected consuls.
60BC Pompey, Crassus and Caesar form an alliance.
59BC Caesar becomes consul.
53BC Crassus dies.
52BC Pompey becomes consul.
48BC Pompey defeated by Caesar in Greece.
44BC Caesar murdered by Brutus and Cassius.

The army

The expansion of Rome was due mostly to the skill and efficiency of its army. The Roman forces were the best disciplined and among the largest in the ancient world. The army had a very strong influence on political life and many politicians were also important soldiers. The structure of the army changed considerably during Rome's history.

The early republican army

During the early republic†, in a military emergency, all property-owning citizens† were summoned to the *Campus Martius* (Field of Mars, god of war). They gathered in groups called centuries, each of 100 men. At first wars only lasted a few days, so it did not matter if men left their farms for a short time.

Richer citizens could afford horses, and so served in the cavalry†.

The poorest fought on the edges of the battle, using stones and farm implements.

The rest fought in a block carrying swords, spears, daggers and shields.

By around 340BC wars further away from Rome meant that people were required to leave their farms for longer periods. Wages were introduced to encourage people to join the army. In a crisis the Romans could raise almost 800,000 men, though these emergency armies were often badly trained. Occasionally even slaves† were brought in to increase the numbers, but this was dangerous as armed slaves could turn against their masters.

Soldiers were grouped into units called legions, each of about 4200 men. Within each legion there were groups of different types of soldier. The structure of individual legions varied. This diagram shows the various fighters, and the way in which they were organized in a typical legion.

Legions were divided into groups called maniples. Each maniple contained 120 men. The maniples fought in a special formation called a *quincunx*, shown below, made up of three ranks of soldiers.

In front of the *triarii* fought a second rank, 10 maniples of *principes*, men armed with plenty of weapons and cylindrical shields.

The gaps in each line were covered by the troops in the line behind.

At the rear of the *quincunx* were 5 maniples (600 men) of very experienced fighters called *triarii*.

Maniple of *triarii*

Maniple of *hastati*

Enemy soldiers

Maniple of *principes*

Velites

The *quincunx* worked well against armies in other formations. First the *hastati* wore out the enemy, then the *principes* moved through to finish the battle. The *triarii* only had to fight if a battle was going badly.

10 maniples of the youngest, poorest soldiers fought separately from the *quincunx*. They were called *velites*.

10 maniples (1200 men) of young soldiers fought at the front. They were called *hastati* because they carried *hastae* (spears).

The later republican army

As the empire grew, the army had to be improved to control Rome's distant enemies. By 100BC the army had been reorganized by a commander called Marius. New laws allowed all citizens to join the legion, whether or not they owned property. Wages were improved, and many men became full-time soldiers. Everyone was given the same weapons and training, so the distinction between rich and poor soldiers disappeared. Most troops fought on foot, but there was also a small cavalry. Legions were extremely well organized because they were made up of many small, highly disciplined groups. The main unit was still the century. Below is a plan of how it was made up.

There were now 80 men in a century rather than 100, because the smaller number was easier to manage.

Century

Each soldier was a member of a *contubernium*, eight men who shared a tent and ate together. There were 10 *contubernia* in a century.

Contubernium

Optio
In charge of each century was a more experienced soldier called a centurion. His second in command was called an *optio*.

Each century also ▶ had a *signifer* (standard-bearer) who carried the century's emblem. He also organized the burial club, a society that soldiers joined to ensure they had a good funeral if they were killed in battle.

◀ So that enemies did not infiltrate the army, each century had a password that was changed each day. The *tesserarius* gave out the new password to the soldiers every morning.

Centuries were grouped into units called cohorts. The cohort became the main tactical unit, replacing the maniple. Ten cohorts made up a legion, the largest fighting group. The exact size of each legion varied from time to time, but the structure of a typical legion, with around 5000 soldiers, is shown below.

◀ Each cohort was led by a junior officer called a *tribunus militum*.

In charge of building ▶ and organizing camps was an experienced soldier, the *praefectus castrorum*.

The legion was led by a senior officer ◀ called a *legatus*.

In each legion, one cohort (the *prima cohors*) was larger than the others. It contained 10 centuries (800 men). Some of these were horseback messengers, cooks or clerks, and did not normally fight.

The other 9 cohorts each contained 6 centuries (480 men), making a total of 4320 legionaries.

Cohort

Century

Ordinary cohorts

Contubernium

Each legion owned ▶ an eagle made of silver, called an *aquila*. It was carried in battle by a soldier called an *aquilifer*. The eagle was a symbol of the legion's power. If the enemy captured it the legion was disbanded.

Other soldiers

Each legion was supported by *auxilia*, non-citizens recruited mostly from the provinces. These soldiers were organized into cohorts of 500 or 1000 men. They were paid less than legionaries, served for longer, and were not as well trained. At the end of their service, however, they received Roman citizenship. They provided forces that legionaries were not trained for, such as cavalry.

A soldier's life

In early republican† times any property-owning man aged between 17 and 46 could be called on to serve in the army. It was seen as a citizen's† duty to protect Rome. Soldiers were not required to fight more than 16 or 17 separate campaigns during their careers, but some liked military service and served continuously. By 100BC most soldiers were full-time professionals.

On entering the army a recruit took an oath of loyalty. At first he swore allegiance to his commander, but later this was replaced by an oath to the emperor†.

Training was hard. Each day new recruits did two sessions of military drill, and the entire legion practised swimming, running, jumping, javelin-throwing and fencing.

Three times a month there were route-marches of 30km (18 miles). The pace was forced at 6.5km (4 miles) or even 8km (5 miles) per hour. Legionaries were trained to build and dismantle camps.

Soldiers were flogged if they misbehaved. If a legion disobeyed its rations were reduced; if mutiny was suspected, every tenth man was executed. The word for this was *decimatio*. It is the origin of the English word decimate, which means to reduce by a tenth.

In difficult countryside carts could not be used to transport equipment. Soldiers had to carry all their belongings, food, tools for digging and building, two heavy wooden stakes for the camp fence, and cooking pots. Because of this soldiers were nicknamed 'the mules of Marius'†.

As well as learning to fight, some soldiers were trained as surveyors, engineers or stonemasons, and supervised the construction of roads, canals and buildings.

Under Caesar† legionaries earned 225 *denarii*† per year. Domitian† increased this to 300 *denarii*. Soldiers had to buy their food, which took about a third of their wages. Meals were simple: cheese, beans, and bread or gruel made of wheat or barley. Soldiers drank water or *posca*, a cheap sour wine.

Until AD5 full-time soldiers served for 20 years. Later this was raised to 25 years. The government knew that retired soldiers could be dangerous, and wanted to keep them peaceful. So discharged veterans were given a sum of money, or a small plot of land to farm.

Uniform and weapons

When a recruit entered the army he was given a uniform. All new garments had to be paid for out of his wages. A soldier's basic outfit varied little according to his rank or status. These pictures show what legionaries wore.

Soldiers carried shields made of wood and leather with an iron rim at the top and bottom. They were about 120cm (48in) by 70cm (28in), and curved.

The sword was about 60cm (2ft) long. It hung from the soldier's belt by his right hand.

Soldiers carried two metal-tipped javelins to throw in battle. They had wooden shafts with a section of soft iron. The iron bent when the spear hit the ground, so the enemy could not throw it back. If the spear hit armour it was impossible to remove.

Scarf to stop the armour scratching the soldier's neck.

In cold weather soldiers were given woollen cloaks.

Vests of fine chain-mail were the most common form of armour.

In colder climates *bracae* (woollen trousers) were also issued.

At first helmets were made of leather. Later, metal was used, to give better protection.

Tunic of wool or linen.

Later, some soldiers wore the *lorica segmentata*, a leather tunic with metal strips attached. This allowed more freedom of movement.

A dagger hung from the left of the soldier's belt.

Groin-guard made of leather and metal.

Heavy sandals studded with nails.

Metal leg-protectors, known as greaves.

Making a camp

During the wars to secure the empire, legions spent many days on the march. When they stopped each night they set up camp, then dismantled it the following morning before moving on. The procedure was highly organized.

The camp was always laid out the same way so everyone knew his part in building it. Josephus, a Jewish priest captured by the Romans in AD67, observed Roman tactics and fighting methods. His book, *The Jewish War*, tells how camps were built.

If the ground was uneven it was levelled off. The camp was marked out as a square.

Injured soldiers were treated in a military hospital (see page 68).

The general's headquarters were at the centre of the camp. This area was also used for meetings, and to house standards and military emblems.

The tents were pitched a long way from the perimeter so that they could not be hit by the enemy's missiles.

The inside of the square was divided into rows, on which the tents were pitched.

A trench was dug around the perimeter. The soil from the ditch was made into a mound, and a fence of stakes was driven into it.

Tents were made of goat- or calf-skin. Each tent housed a *contubernium*, a group of eight men.

Each centurion† had his own tent, at the end of the row of tents of his century.

Branches were woven through the stakes, so from outside the fence looked like a wall. Lookout towers and artillery machines were placed on it.

Streets crossed the camp, dividing it into quarters.

17

Roads

The Romans developed their system of roads out of military necessity. In the early years of Rome's expansion, the army could march from the city to defend the frontiers in a few hours. As the empire grew, however, it became vital to move troops and supplies quickly over very long distances.

The first major road, the *Via Appia*, was begun in 312BC. It stretched south from Rome to Capua and took over 100 years to build. 900 years after its completion, the historian Procopius called it one of the great sights of the world. He noted that despite its age, none of the stones had broken or worn thin.

The *Via Appia* was the first link in a network that eventually stretched over 85,000km (50,000 miles) and reached every corner of the empire (see map below). Much later, the remains of these routes formed the basis of Europe's modern roads and railway lines.

The *Via Appia* as it is today.

This map shows the network of Roman roads.

Extent of Roman territory

As well as helping the movement of troops, roads brought other changes. Merchants followed armies to sell to the troops, and later to the inhabitants of the new provinces. Trade flourished, and people and goods could quickly reach distant parts of the empire. So roads helped to unite the provinces, as well as to keep them under control.

Travelling

This roadside scene has been reconstructed using information from Roman manuscripts, pictures and remains. We know what Roman vehicles looked like, and also know their names, but it is not easy to match the two. Two-wheeled carriages, used in towns, included the *carpentum* and the more lightweight *cisium*. There were also larger, four-wheeled vehicles like the *raeda*, which could carry a whole family, and the *carruca*, which had enough room to sleep in.

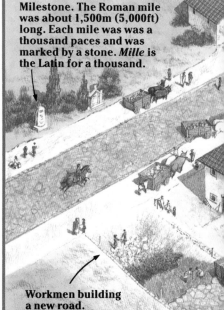

Milestone. The Roman mile was about 1,500m (5,000ft) long. Each mile was was a thousand paces and was marked by a stone. *Mille* is the Latin for a thousand.

Workmen building a new road.

Building a road

When planning a road, Roman surveyors looked for the shortest, straightest, flattest route. To find this they took sights from one high point to another. They probably did this by lighting fires, flares or beacons, observing carrier pigeons, or using a *groma* (see page 72). Once the route had been planned, the turf and trees were cleared in preparation. Then a trench was dug about 1m (3½feet) deep and filled with layers of stone. To prevent puddles (which would crack the road if they froze), the surface was built with a raised curve called a camber, and ditches were dug to drain water away.

Stone slabs (if stone was available locally).

Camber

Gravel or small flints rammed down tight.

Groma

Drainage ditch

Smaller stones, sometimes bound with cement.

Large stones, wedged tightly together.

Minor roads were 3m to 4.5m (10ft) wide, major ones up to 7.7m (25ft).

Roman roads are sometimes steeper than ours. This is because soldiers preferred a short steep climb to a long trudge round a hill.

Taberna

Soldiers

There were post stations on main roads, between 6 and 15 Roman miles apart. They were part of the *cursus publicus*, a postal service set up for government use only. Horse-riders took official messages by relay from one station to the next.

Chariot carrying government mail.

Local workpeople could find food and drink in a *taberna* (tavern). Tradesmen also used these as places to sell their goods, and towns often grew up around them.

Coach taking passengers to the next city.

Farmer taking vegetables to the next town.

Travellers could stay at state-controlled guest-houses called *mansiones*. These were built every 15 Roman miles or so. Some *mansiones* were huge, but they were not always very comfortable.

Mansio

Where the route came to rivers, or valleys that were too steep for men and mules to climb, bridges or viaducts† had to be built. Many of these can still be seen today, and some are still in use, such as this one which spans the river at Alcantara in Spain.

Most Roman vehicles had wheels set about 143cm (60 in) apart. This width (or gauge) became standard once ruts had been worn in the roads. No-one wanted to travel with only one wheel in a rut, so they built their carts at the standard gauge.

Sometimes, instead of a ditch, earth was dug and piled into a mound, with foundation stones on top. This kind of road was called an *agger* and was up to 15m (50ft) wide and 1.5m (5ft) high. *Aggers* were probably built as boundaries or to impress local people.

Ships and shipping

Unlike the Greeks or Phoenicians†, the Romans had no tradition of seafaring. During the early republic they only had primitive shipping forces. However for the first Punic war (264-241 BC; see page 8), they had to acquire naval power quickly. They found an abandoned Carthaginian warship, and built 100 copies of it in 60 days; eventually they had over 200 ships. After defeating Carthage the Romans dominated the Mediterranean Sea. They built a merchant fleet, and sea trade flourished. Later they also had a navy that patrolled the seas to prevent piracy.

Warships and naval tactics

There is little information about Roman warships because no wrecks have been found. We know from Roman books that they were called *quinqueremes*. Some historians think that these ships had five banks of oars. Others say this would have made them impossible to row, and think it more likely that each oar was pulled by five men. These diagrams show warships and their weapons.

The spiked drawbridge, called a *corvus*, was lowered onto enemy ships so that soldiers could climb onto their opponents' decks to fight.

At its fastest a warship could travel 19km (12 miles) per hour. Each ship had about 300 oarsmen.

120 soldiers were carried on deck to fight.

Other ships were equipped with underwater rams. These were used to break holes in the enemy's ships.

Triremes

After the Punic wars there were no major naval battles, but the Romans kept a fleet of warships called *triremes*. Later, during the civil wars between Mark Antony† and Octavian† (c.33-30BC; see overleaf) each side built up huge navies. 900 *triremes* fought at the Battle of Actium. After his victory Octavian set up the first permanent navy to guard the coasts of Italy. A typical *trireme* is shown in this relief.

A *trireme* had three banks of oars, pulled by slaves below deck.

A *trireme* was lighter and narrower than a *quinquereme*, and therefore easier to manoeuvre.

The crocodile on the front suggests that the ship is from a fleet based on the Nile.

Harbours

When the Romans began using larger merchant ships (see opposite) they needed large, deep harbours. Rome was served by a port called Ostia at the mouth of the Tiber. Claudius† built a vast new port, Portus, nearby. Harbours were also built elsewhere in the empire. Towns grew up around them because they became trading centres. This is what a provincial port might have looked like.

Barges took goods inland along rivers or canals, because many ships were too wide for this journey.

Large merchant ships brought supplies from other parts of the empire.

Naval ships sometimes docked in harbours.

Merchant ships

After the rule of Augustus†, the Romans had a vast fleet of merchant ships to carry goods all over the Mediterranean, and as far as Africa and India. Ships had to be sturdy enough for frequent journeys, because Romans relied on imported goods for much of their food. Wrecks of merchant ships have been found which show how they were built.

The frame was usually made of oak, and the planks of pine, cypress or elder. The hull was often coated in lead to stop the wood from rotting.

Then floors and frames were fitted to make the hold. This was where the cargo was carried.

Hull

Wooden nail

Each plank was attached to the ones above and below it, and to the hull, by a special joint. This gave the boat extra strength.

First the keel was placed in position.

Then planks were attached one by one to posts at either end of the boat. These formed the hull.

Merchant ships were wider than warships to enable them to carry large loads.

A cargo ship

Roman paintings, carvings and wrecks reveal what cargo ships were like. They varied in size. Remains have been found of small vessels about 18m (60ft) long and 5m (17ft) wide, but the cargo area of some wrecks measures at least 30m (100ft) by 9m (30ft). Ships carried all kinds of goods – such as *amphorae* of oil and wine, or sacks of grain – over large distances.

Top sail

Central mast

The ship relied on sail power when at sea.

The ends of ships were often elaborately carved.

Main sail

Ships could achieve speeds of up to 7km per hour (over 4 miles per hour).

The oars were for steering.

Steering sail

Navigation

Roman sailors had no instruments to help them find their way, but they quickly learned many routes across the Mediterranean. There were books that told sailors the best routes and best times to travel. We know from these that navigators did not need to keep the coastline in sight as they travelled.

To calculate his position, a captain looked at the sun, moon and stars. He judged his progress by studying the direction and speed of the wind. There were lighthouses at important harbours. The most famous of these, the Pharos at Alexandria, used huge metal plates to reflect the lights of a fire. It stood over 130m (100ft) high, and was one of the wonders of the ancient world.

From republic to Empire

After Caesar's death (see page 13) Brutus† and Cassius fled from Rome, realizing they could not restore the republic†. Instead, one of the consuls†, Mark Antony, tried to take Caesar's place. However many senators disliked him. One of them, Cicero†, made speeches opposing Antony and persuaded the Senate to declare him an outlaw. Antony was dismissed and replaced by another consul.

Coin with head of Antony

In the meantime, Caesar's adopted son, Octavian, formed an army made up of men who had formerly fought for Caesar. He gave control of these troops to the Senate, and they defeated Antony at Mutina in northern Italy. Antony fled to Gaul. The consuls were killed in battle, leaving Octavian as the most likely person to take command.

Busts of Octavian and his wife Livia†

Octavian wanted revenge for Caesar's death. The Senate refused to support him, so he made a pact with Antony and his ally, Lepidus. The three men led an army on Rome, forcing the Senate to give them official powers for five years. Thousands of people, including Cicero, were killed by Octavian's troops. In 42BC Octavian and Antony defeated Brutus and Cassius at Philippi in Macedonia.

Lepidus soon retired, leaving Octavian and Antony in command. They split Rome's territory into two. Antony took the eastern part and Octavian the west, as shown on this map.

Antony's territory
Octavian's territory

Antony lived in Egypt for ten years with his lover Cleopatra, the Egyptian queen. He seemed to be building a private empire for himself. Meanwhile Octavian defeated his enemies in western Europe, and became accepted by the Senate and the Roman people. But relations between him and Antony deteriorated. War broke out, and in 31BC he defeated Antony in a sea battle at Actium.

This gem depicts Octavian as Neptune, the god of the sea. It was carved to celebrate his victory over Mark Antony at the Battle of Actium.

Octavian takes power

Octavian claimed Egypt for himself, and became the sole leader of the Roman world. In 27BC he offered to return control of the state to the Senate and the people. However he knew that the Senate could not accept his offer because it depended on him to maintain order. The Senate gave Octavian command of three provinces: Syria, Spain and Gaul. These areas contained most of the army, so he retained military power while appearing to want to give it up for the sake of the republic†.

As a result Octavian became the most powerful Roman of all. He was given a new name, Augustus ('revered one'), and has been known by this title ever since. He was the first Roman emperor, though he himself did not use this title. The period of Roman history from his rule onwards is known as the Empire, to distinguish it from the republic before it.

This cameo† shows the head of Augustus.

Key dates

44BC Death of Caesar.

43BC Octavian, Antony and Lepidus form an alliance and seize power in Rome.

c.33BC Growing hostility between Octavian and Antony.

31BC Octavian defeats Antony and Cleopatra at the Battle of Actium.

30BC Antony and Cleopatra commit suicide. Octavian seizes Egypt and becomes sole leader of the Roman world.

27BC Octavian becomes emperor and takes the name Augustus.

The rule of Augustus, 27BC-AD14

With his new power, Augustus began looking for solutions to his various political problems. He realized that further civil wars would only weaken the empire more and leave it open to threat from outside. So he tried to make his own position safe in order to maintain a firm leadership.

Knowing that too many organized troops could be turned against him, Augustus cut the number of legions† from 60 to 28. He used the vast wealth of Egypt to pay off retired soldiers, who were settled in colonies all over Italy.

Retired soldier

Praetorian guardsmen

To protect himself, Augustus formed a division of soldiers called the Praetorian Guard. These highly paid troops were intended to guard the Emperor, and were stationed in Rome and throughout Italy.

Under Augustus, rebellious parts of Spain and the Alps were brought under control. The empire was expanded along the Rhine and Danube rivers. The map below shows the extent of the empire at the end of Augustus's rule.

Augustus ruled cleverly and successfully. He formed a system of government in which the Senate and the emperor worked together. This brought peace after years of civil war, and turned a troubled republic into a stable and prosperous empire. When he died in AD14, few people could remember a republican government that had been worth preserving, so the idea of restoring a republic slowly died out.

Tiberius AD14-37

Augustus had no son of his own, and wanted one of his grandsons or his nephew to take his place, but they all died young. Eventually he had to name his step-son Tiberius as his successor. The two men ruled together for the last ten years of Augustus's reign. Augustus

Statue of Tiberius

disliked him, but Tiberius was a fine soldier and an experienced administrator.

At first Tiberius ruled well. He took Augustus's advice and did not try to expand the empire. But he was terrified of being assassinated. At first there was no evidence of a plot against him, but Sejanus, the commander of the Praetorian Guard, took advantage of his fears.

In AD26 Sejanus persuaded Tiberius to move to the island of Capri for his own safety. For the rest of his rule, the Senate had to consult him by letter before it could make decisions. In AD31 Tiberius found out that Sejanus was planning to depose him. He revealed this to the Senate and Sejanus and his family were executed. This left Tiberius mentally disturbed. He passed a treason law and prosecuted over 100 leading figures. 65 of these were executed or committed suicide.

Gaius (Caligula) AD37-41

Gaius is often known as Caligula, a nickname he was given as a child because of the soldier's boots (*caligae*) he wore. After a few months in power he had an illness which appears to have left him deranged. He claimed to be a god and tried to have his horse elected consul. He married his sister and later murdered her.

Caligula was extremely extravagant. He financed his spending by forcing rich men to bequeath him their wealth. This, and his cruelty, made him unpopular and he was murdered by a group of officers from the Praetorian Guard.

The early Empire

Claudius AD41-54

Coin with head of Claudius

Claudius was Tiberius's nephew. A childhood disease had left him crippled, frail and nervous. His family and the Senate regarded him as stupid. Because of this everyone thought that he was not suitable to be emperor. After Gaius's murder, however, the Praetorian Guard† found Claudius hiding in the imperial palace. They dragged him off, hailing him as the new emperor, while the Senate was discussing restoring the republic. The senators always resented Claudius because he had been appointed against their will.

Claudius was in fact highly intelligent and wise. He devoted his rule to improving the civil service and extending the empire. He annexed Mauretania and Thrace, and ordered the invasion of Britain. He married four times. His last wife was his niece, Aggripina†. It is thought that she poisoned him so that Nero, her son by a previous marriage, could become emperor.

Nero AD54-68

Nero was only 16 when he became emperor. For the first years of his rule he was guided by tutors (including the writer Seneca†) and ruled sensibly. However, he soon became tyrannical. In AD59 he had his mother, his wife and Claudius's son Britannicus murdered, as well as several advisors. Soon, anyone who opposed him was killed.

Nero liked taking part in theatrical shows, races and games. Many Romans thought his behaviour was very undignified.

In AD64 a fire devastated Rome. It was rumoured that Nero had started it so that he could build a new, more beautiful city in its place. To avert unpopularity, Nero blamed the Christians† for the fire, and had many of them burned or thrown to the beasts. This only made him more unpopular.

According to the Roman historian Suetonius†, Nero sang and played the lyre while Rome burned.

There were many plots against Nero. In AD68 the army rebelled against him and various commanders tried to seize power. Nero was eventually forced to leave Rome, and he committed suicide. He was the last emperor of Augustus's dynasty.

AD69: the year of the four emperors

After Nero's death, an army commander called Galba took power, helped by the Praetorian Guard. But he did not pay the guardsmen enough to win their loyalty. They soon turned against him, had him murdered, and replaced him with Otho, the governor of a province in Spain. Hearing this, the legions on the Rhine declared their own general, Vitellius, emperor. They marched on Rome and defeated Otho at Cremona. Then legions on the Danube decided their own general, Vespasian, should become emperor. He marched on Rome and killed Vitellius and his followers.

Coin with head of Vespasian

Vespasian (AD69-79) and the Flavian Dynasty

Vespasian knew there would be civil war if he did not establish good relations with the Senate. He achieved this, and the Senate granted him imperial power. In addition, he had two adult sons to take over after his death, so he had a strong line of succession. Vespasian ruled well and gave citizenship† to many people in the provinces†. His full name was Titus Flavius Vespasianus, and he and his descendants are known as the Flavian Dynasty.

Vespasian ordered the building of the Colosseum in Rome. This is how it looks today.

Titus AD79-81

Titus was Vespasian's son. He is remembered for his capture of Jerusalem (see page 65) in AD70. This was commemorated by an arch in the *forum* at Rome. Titus became emperor in AD79.

The arch of Titus

Domitian AD81-96

Bust of Domitian

Domitian, Titus's younger brother, was an efficient but arrogant emperor. He despised the Senate and never consulted it. He became unpopular and there were frequent plots against him. His rule became tyrannical, with frequent treason trials and executions. He was assassinated in AD96.

This was probably the last point at which the Romans could have restored a republican government. But the Senate, knowing that Rome needed a strong leader, chose a lawyer called Nerva to replace Domitian. Nerva was the first of a group of rulers known as the Five Good Emperors.

Nerva AD96-98

Nerva ruled successfully and diplomatically. When the Praetorian Guard was indignant at having no say in choosing the emperor, Nerva eased the situation by adopting a famous soldier called Trajan as his son, partner and successor. This started a new method of imperial succession. After Nerva each emperor, who took the title Augustus, carefully chose a younger colleague called the Caesar as his heir. When the Augustus died, the Caesar took his position and title, and then chose his own Caesar.

The imperial succession:

Nerva

The Augustus chose a Caesar to succeed him.

The Caesar took over and became the Augustus.

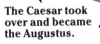

Trajan

He then chose a new Caesar to succeed him

Hadrian

Nerva treated the Senate with great respect, and this trend was followed by the next four emperors. Gradually senators were chosen from all over the empire, and many non-Italians became senior officials. Nerva also arranged low-interest loans for farmers. The interest from these was used to support orphans and poor children.

Trajan AD98-117

Under Trajan the empire reached its largest extent (see pages 26-27) after his conquest of large areas of the Middle East. His campaigns in Dacia (modern Romania) are recorded in a series of sculptures on the pillar in Rome known as Trajan's Column.

Trajan's column

Hadrian AD117-138

Hadrian spent more than half his rule touring the provinces. After deciding that the empire was too large he gave up the new territories in the East (except Dacia). Many of his reforms improved the organization of the empire. For example he decreed that senators and *equites*† should receive special training in state administration.

Hadrian ordered the building of fortified barriers to protect the empire. These were put up in Britain (see pages 28-29) and in Germany.

Hadrian's Wall

Antoninus Pius AD138-161

While Antoninus Pius was in power, Rome was seen to be at the height of its wealth and power. But this prosperity aroused the envy of the barbarians†, and of the poor, who were neglected.

Marcus Aurelius AD161-180

Marcus Aurelius spent most of his rule at the frontiers, trying to keep barbarians out. To do this he had to enlarge the army and raise taxes to cover the cost. During his rule a plague killed thousands of people. For the first time people began to doubt that Rome was all-powerful.

This statue of Marcus Aurelius once stood on the Capitoline Hill.

Key dates: the first emperors

27BC-AD14 Augustus	**AD69-79** Vespasian
AD14-37 Tiberius	**AD79-81** Titus
AD37-41 Gaius (Caligula)	**AD81-96** Domitian
AD41-54 Claudius	**AD96-98** Nerva
AD54-68 Nero	**AD98-117** Trajan
AD64 Great fire of Rome	**AD117-138** Hadrian
AD69 Year of the four emperors	**AD138-161** Antoninus Pius
	AD161-180 Marcus Aurelius

The administration of the empire

Roman territory was divided into areas called provinces. These were governed locally by senators representing the republic†, or, later, the emperor. When a province was made part of the empire, a special provincial law was drawn up for it. This differed from the law in Rome, because it took local customs into account and set local levels of taxation. After this, provincials were mostly left to govern themselves. This map* indicates the extent of the empire at its largest, under Trajan (AD98-117), and shows how it was organized.

Before it was conquered by the Romans, much of western Europe was inhabited by rural tribes and nomads†. The Romans built large towns there, partly to make it easier to govern and partly because they believed urban life was a good thing. Most towns roughly followed the plan shown here.

Barbarians

Outside the empire were many rural tribes. The Romans saw them as inferior, brutal and uncivilized, referring to them as barbarians. Many barbarian tribes threatened the empire's security. Some wanted to regain territory that the Romans had taken from them, others wanted to steal cattle and other goods. To keep invaders out, the Romans built walls along some of their borders. These are shown as blue lines.

Caledonia
BRITANNIA
GERMANIA
Germania inferior
Belgica
Rhaetia
Noricum
Dacia
Germania superior
Pannonia
Lugdunensis
GALLIA
Alpes Penninae
Illyricum
Atlantic Ocean
Aquitania
Alpes Cottiae
Adriatic Sea
Dalmatia
Narbonensis
Rome
Macedonia
Alpes Maritimae
Corsica
ITALIA
Epirus
Tarraconensis
Sardinia
GRAECI
HISPANIA
Sicilia
Achaea
Lusitania
Mediterranean Sea
Baetica
Africa
MAURETANIA
Numidia
Caesariensis
Tingitana
AFRICA

The imperial army

When Augustus took power in 31BC the army consisted of 60 legions†. He cut this number to 28, and used them to protect the empire's frontiers. Later emperors varied this number slightly, but there were always around 30. Hadrian† began recruiting soldiers from areas in which they would be stationed. For example German troops were recruited to serve in Germany.

German soldier

Gradually the army became inefficient. Some later emperors thought the legions might turn against them, and to prevent this they gave soldiers special privileges and frequent pay increases. This made generals too powerful, and caused discipline problems. It became harder to recruit soldiers within the empire, because fewer people wanted to join the army. Sometimes the Romans recruited barbarians to defend frontiers, but their loyalty could not be guaranteed.

For a note about the projection of this map, see page 3.

Most eastern Mediterranean countries had a civilization much older than Rome's. Many had been influenced by Greek civilization. They were urban societies, accustomed to central government and paying taxes.

Many Roman buildings were copied from Greek temples like this one.

Government in the provinces

Under the republic, the Senate† appointed governors for each province. They were chosen from retiring *praetores*† and consuls†, and served for one to three years. Governors had various duties. They commanded the army in the area, ensuring that frontiers were safe and maintaining law and order. They organized the collection of local taxes, which were used to pay the army stationed in the area. They also acted as judges for important trials. Governors were paid expenses, but no wages. Many, believing they would not be found out by the Senate, used their power to extort money from locals. For this reason they were often disliked.

Caspian Sea

Black Sea   Armenia

Moesia
Thracia   Pontus

                    Assyria

Cappadocia

Bithynia   Mesopotamia

Galatia   Babylonia

Asia   Cilicia   Syria

Lycia

            Cyprus
Pamphylia   Judaea
        Phoenicia

Aegean Sea

Creta

                    ◻ **Fortified border**

            Arabia

Cyrenaica

        Aegyptus

Barbarian soldier

Under Constantine† the frontiers were guarded by peasant soldiers who had settled near forts. To support them Constantine organized mobile armies, nearly all cavalry, which were stationed near the borders. This policy worked for over a century, but finally the army disintegrated and the barbarians moved in (see pages 78-79).

The governor was helped by a *quaestor*, a junior official who organized the finances of the province and the collection of taxes.

There were were also three or four lieutenants (called *legati*) who carried out the governor's orders on a day-to-day basis.

Civil servants called *apparitores* worked as clerks and messengers. They came mostly from Rome, rather than the province itself.

In imperial times the Senate lost much of its power in the provinces, because the emperor took control of the dangerous areas by the frontiers. Under Augustus only the legion in Africa remained under senatorial control. After this, though certain areas passed from the emperor's control to the Senate's from time to time, the emperor always held supreme power in matters of provincial government. The emperor could not manage all the provinces personally, so he sent senators to govern for him.

In the emperor's provinces financial affairs were not managed by *quaestores*, but by the emperor's own agents called *procuratores Augusti*. They reported directly to the emperor, so were a useful check on the governor's behaviour.

Sieges and fortifications

The Romans were very determined fighters. They even conquered towns that were protected by high walls or built on clifftops. Sometimes the Romans simply surrounded towns. The inhabitants, unable to get in or out, were slowly starved of food and had to surrender. This took a long time, however, so the Romans invented techniques to break down defences more quickly. They also used heavy weapons, or artillery, called *tormenta*. These machines could fire missiles over long distances. Ropes made of horsehair or human hair were twisted and stretched so that when released they shot missiles with great force. This is what a siege might have looked like.

First the Romans surrounded the town.

Some soldiers tried to break holes in the walls.

Others built siege-works, wooden scaffolding and platforms that enabled them to climb the walls.

Most effective of all were siege towers. They were taller than the city walls and could be built away from the fortifications.

When finished, the siege tower was pushed up to the walls and soldiers climbed up inside. A drawbridge was lowered so that the soldiers could enter the city.

If soldiers wanted to approach the wall without being hit by the enemy's arrows, they grouped together and covered themselves completely with their shields. This formation was called a *testudo* (tortoise).

Large stationary crossbows were used to fire spears. Sometimes burning rags were attached to the tips.

The *onager* was a larger, heavy catapult, capable of firing massive rocks over 500 metres (1600ft).

Permanent fortifications

Hadrian† wanted permanent frontiers at the borders of the empire. Walls were built in Germany, Numidia and Britain. The one in Britain, known as Hadrian's Wall, is the best preserved. It runs for nearly 130km (80 miles) from the River Tyne to the River Solway, and was mainly built between AD122 and AD129. It was not only a barrier, like a city wall. It also had a political function, enabling the Romans to control the tribes to the north. This is a reconstruction of part of Hadrian's Wall.

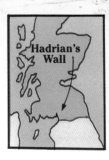

Hadrian's Wall

Built into the wall, roughly equal distances apart, were 16 large forts. Each of these housed an auxiliary cohort of 1000 men, or a cavalry division of 500 men and their horses.

The wall was built by the soldiers in the three British legions. The legions were responsible for the upkeep and administration of the wall, but it was actually staffed by *auxilia* (see page 15).

Maintaining frontiers

When legions settled at frontiers they set up permanent camps, laid out much like the temporary ones that soldiers built when they were on the march (see page 17). Legionary camps held about 5000 people, and each followed a similar plan so that soldiers could find their way around wherever they were. At first the soldiers lived in tents, later in wooden huts. In the 2nd century AD they began building forts out of stone, like the one shown here.

1 *Principium* (headquarters)

2 *Praetorium* (commander's house)

3 Barrack blocks

4 Granaries

5 Drill hall

6 Workshop

7 Houses for officers

8 Barrack blocks for first cohort†

9 Cavalry's accommodation

10 Houses for centurions† of first cohort

11 House for senior centurion

12 *Valetudinarium* (hospital)

Soldiers often settled near forts when they retired, so towns grew up around them. Remains of private houses and taverns have been found near forts in Britain.

At intervals of one Roman mile (1500m or 5000ft) were 79 towers called milecastles. Each one contained accommodation for a few troops.

The wall was over 4.5m (15ft) high, and in places 3m (10ft) thick.

Milecastle

The parapet along the top protected troops as they walked along.

South of the road ran another ditch, called the *vallum*.

Between every pair of milecastles were two turrets, roughly 500m (1600ft) apart. These were used as lookouts, and for sending signals along the wall.

A road ran behind the wall, linking the forts.

A ditch in front of the wall was further defence against invaders.

Roman towns

Early Roman towns had no particular plan or design, unlike many Greek cities which were built on a grid pattern with streets at right angles to each other. This idea had been introduced about 450BC by the Greek town planner Hippodamus.

When the Romans occupied the Greek cities in southern Italy around 250BC, they quickly adopted the grid pattern for themselves. To it they added the features of the Roman town – the *forum*, basilicas, amphitheatres†, baths, drains and water systems. This is a reconstruction of a typical Roman town. The basic features became standard throughout the empire.

Many towns in the provinces that existed before the Romans occupied them had defensive walls. During the early empire, when these towns were protected by the army, walls were no longer needed. New towns were even forbidden to build them. Later, however, when invaders threatened the empire, earthworks were permitted. Many of these were later made into stone walls.

Library

The *thermae*, or public baths (see pages 60-61).

Gymnasium

Prosperous towns were extremely crowded and busy, with few open spaces. The number of apartment blocks caused a high density of population, particularly as expansion was limited by the town walls.

Most towns of any size had a theatre (see page 56) and an amphitheatre (see page 59).

Roman towns always had many inns (*tabernae*), snack bars (*thermopolia*) and bakeries (*pistrina*).

A town usually had four or more gates, with roads to neighbouring towns running through them.

Roman towns have been occupied and rebuilt over the centuries, so it is difficult to see the grid pattern in their remains. However it can be seen clearly in the ruins of Timgad in North Africa, because the town was deserted after Roman times.

The roads outside the city were lined with tombs and graves. Burials were not allowed inside the walls.

There were so many traffic jams that some towns barred wheeled traffic, apart from builders' wagons, from their streets during daylight hours.

Aqueducts (see page 73) provided the town's water supply.

Insulae

The *insulae* contained private dwellings. These were either the private houses of the rich, called *domus* (see page 34), or the large apartment blocks (also called *insulae*, see page 35).

Many towns had two main streets, one running north to south, the other running east to west. The other roads also ran at right angles to each other, leaving square spaces between them, called *insulae* (islands).

Domus

There were usually temples to the many Roman gods (see pages 62-65).

Hygiene

Gutter

Stepping stones (so that people could avoid getting their feet wet).

Sewer

The town's waste was carried in sewage systems under the streets. There were gutters along the edge of the streets, so that rainwater could run through them into the sewers.

The forum

The *forum* was a large open space, used as a market place. It was normally built at the point where the two main streets crossed.

On the fourth side was a basilica, a large building used as a law court and for other public functions.

Warehouses

The *forum* was usually surrounded on three sides by a covered walkway which contained shops and offices.

Statue of the town's patron god.

Fountain

Jugglers and tumblers entertained passers-by.

Traders sold goods from stalls and carts.

In or near the basilica was the *curia* (town hall). The *ordo* (town council) met here. The council was responsible for the administration of the town.

The city of Rome

From a small hilltop settlement, Rome grew into the largest, most magnificent city in the ancient world. The empire's wealth and power was reflected in the capital city's public buildings and monuments. Many emperors wanted to leave their mark on the city's landscape, so they commissioned new buildings to compete in size and splendour with earlier ones. But Rome was also highly overcrowded, and there were many squalid tenements. At its largest the ancient city had well over a million inhabitants. This is a reconstruction of Rome as it might have looked in imperial times.

Temple of Serapis

Trajan's market

Trajan's temple

Forum of Augustus

Trajan's column

Forum of Vespasian

Trajan's forum

Senate House

Arch of Severus

Basilica Julia

Temple of Jupiter Capitolinus

Theatre of Marcellus

Temple of Augustus

Temple of Vesta

Temple of Aesculapius

Palace of Augustus

Circus Maximus

How Rome grew

Forum

River Tiber

Servian Wall

Circus Maximus

Forum

Colosseum

Aurelian Wall

At first Rome was a small group of settlements occupying 7 hills by the River Tiber. By the 4th century BC the city had reached the extent of the Servian Wall, built in 387BC.

In AD64 Rome was devastated by a fire. There was extensive rebuilding and the city grew rapidly. The suburbs expanded far outside the Servian Wall and across the River Tiber.

In AD271-5 the Aurelian Wall was built. It roughly marked the full extent of Ancient Rome, though the city continued to expand across the Tiber for some years.

Baths of Constantine

Basilicas, like the one shown above, were huge public buildings used as law courts and offices. After the rise of Christianity (see page 65) many basilicas were turned into churches.

After the fire in AD64 Nero† built a palace called the Golden House, and put this immense statue of himself in its grounds. The palace was torn down when he was deposed, and the statue's head was replaced with that of the god Apollo.

Basilica of Maxentius

Temple of Venus and Rome

Statue of Apollo

Colosseum

Baths of Trajan

Temple of Jupiter Stator

Arch of Constantine

Ludus Magnus

Aqueduct of Nero

Temple of the Divine Claudius

Triumphal arches, like the arch of Constantine† (above) were built to celebrate battle victories. There were several arches in Rome, and many similar ones in the provinces.

The Temple of the Divine Claudius was built in AD54, when Claudius† was declared a god. There were temples all over the city dedicated to the many Roman deities.

Town houses

By the time of the later republic, most townspeople lived in large apartment blocks called *insulae*. Each individual apartment was called a *cenaculum*. Only very rich people could afford to live in a private house, or *domus*. A survey of Rome in AD350 listed 1790 *domus* and 46,602 *insulae*, though elsewhere the proportion of private houses may have been higher.

A domus

Most town houses were variations of the same basic plan. Some, like this one, had rooms on a second storey, but this was not very common.

Guests were received in the *atrium*. The word comes from the word *ater*, meaning black. In early times the *atrium* was the only room, and it was blackened by smoke from the fire.

The rooms at the front opened on to the street. They were often rented out as shops.

The tiled roof of the *atrium* † sloped down to an opening called a *compluvium*. In cold weather it could be covered by canvas.

Rain collected in a shallow pool called the *impluvium*. When the water rose to a certain level, it was piped to a tank underneath the house.

The family lived in the rooms at the back of the house between the *atrium* and the garden.

Tablinum (study)

In warm climates windows were left open, or covered with wooden shutters, animal skin or layers of semi-transparent stone. Glass windows were rare.

The *lararium*, a shrine to the household gods, was kept in the garden or the *atrium*.

Kitchen (see page 40)

The dining room was called a *triclinium* (see pages 38-39).

Most houses had no bathrooms, because in every town there were many public bath-houses (see pages 60-61).

A walled garden like this was called a *peristylium*.

Central heating

The Romans developed their central heating system, called the hypocaust, in the first century AD. In warm climates, like Italy, it was used mainly in bath-houses, but in colder parts of the empire it could be found in town houses and country villas. This diagram shows how the hypocaust system worked.

When the house was being built, fire-grates were constructed in the basement. The floor at ground level was supported by pillars of concrete or brick.

Fires were lit in the grates. The warm air circulated under the floors and through ducts in the walls. Once warm, the pillars retained their heat for a long time.

Floor

We cannot tell how the Romans adjusted the heat, apart from building up the fire or damping it down.

Fire-grate

Pillars

Insulae

Some apartments were luxurious and spacious, while others were cramped and squalid. They could have many rooms, or only one. Limits were imposed on the height to which *insulae* could be built – normally only four or five storeys were allowed.

Poorer tenants lived in the upper storeys, which were built of wood. The rooms were smaller and often in very bad condition.

Landlords often built extra rooms so that they could make more money, but these were often badly constructed of cheap materials. This made buildings very unsafe, and many collapsed.

Woodburning braziers were the only form of heating used, but these were a great fire risk and there were no chimneys.

The *insulae* had no internal drains, so people threw their waste into gutters in the streets.

Rich occupants often had several well-furnished, comfortable rooms to live in.

Few *insulae* had their own toilets. People had to use public lavatories like this.

Cooking was impossible in the flats, so people ate cold snacks, or went to inns and bars for their meals.

The lower storeys, usually built of stone, were for richer tenants.

There was no running water, but people fetched water from the many public fountains nearby.

The rooms at street level were sometimes let as shops or taverns. People rarely lived in the ground-floor rooms of *insulae*.

The storeys were connected by a staircase.

Firefighting

Fire was a constant risk in Rome, because of the hot, dry climate, the overcrowded conditions, and the use of open fires in wooden buildings. Augustus† set up a fire service for Rome. There were seven brigades, called *vigiles*, each with 1000 men. The city was divided into 14 regions and each brigade was responsible for two of them. These fire brigades were copied in other towns, though on a smaller scale.

Simple hand-held pumps were used to fight small fires, but they could only deliver a small amount of water.

Sponges and leather buckets were used to dampen undamaged walls to stop the fire spreading.

Furniture

Roman houses were quite sparsely furnished. Apart from the *atrium* and the *tablinum* (see page 34), many rooms were too small to hold much furniture. Most surviving Roman furniture is made of marble or metal, but this may be misleading. Wooden furniture may have been more usual, but most of it would have since decayed.

A back, head, or foot-board might be added, depending on the purpose of the bed.

Cushions and mattresses were filled with wool or feathers.

Webbing of leather or cloth.

A blanket was the on covering.

Beds

Beds and couches were important items of furniture. They were used in studies and dining rooms as well as bedrooms, in place of sofas.

Luxurious bed-frames were often inlaid with precious metals.

Some other kinds of Roman be

Chairs

Scamnum

Folding chair

Sella

Bisellium

A Roman stool was called a *scamnum*. Stools usually had three legs and a round wooden top, or four legs and a square or rectangular top, often made of bronze.

A *sella* was a chair with four legs, arms, and no back. A larger version, the *bisellium*, was used by important people. The Romans also had folding chairs.

The *cathedra* had a high, curved back, and was usually used by old people. It was often made of wicker. A judge sat on a *cathedra* with a hard back.

Tables

Tables varied a lot in price, and Romans were prepared to spend large sums of money on them. As the Romans frequently ate outside, marble or stone tables were common.

Marble table

Table made of metal and wood

The one-legged table, called a *monopodium*, was particularly expensive. The central support could be carved in ivory, or be made of elaborately cast metal. Precious, rare woods were sometimes used for the tops.

Storage

For storage, the Romans used heavy chests and cupboards.

Heating and lighting

The Romans used oil lamps and tapers to light their houses. For heating they used small bronze braziers, or enclosed heaters which looked more like modern stoves. For fuel they used wood, charcoal, or coke, a refined form of coal.

To make a taper, the stalk of a marsh plant like papyrus was dipped in a vat of wax or tallow. The tapers were then twisted together into a sort of rope.

A brazier

Thousands of oil lamps have survived. They were made of terracotta† or metal, and burned vegetable oil (from olives, nuts or sesame) or fish oil. This produced a light similar to a candle.

The wick protruded through a nozzle at the front.

Lamps were long and flat, with a handle at the back.

There were also hanging lamps with chains and hooks.

Lanterns were widely used. The flame was protected by pieces of horn, or animal bladder. Later lanterns were made of glass.

Decorations

The Romans were more interested in how houses looked inside than how they appeared from the outside. While many town houses looked drab from the street, their interiors were lavishly decorated with wall paintings and mosaics. At first the styles and techniques were adopted from the Greeks. Many Romans employed Greeks to decorate their rooms, because they were thought to be the best artists. This reconstruction shows decorators at work in a Roman house.

Artists began painting pictures on the walls while the plaster was still damp. Paintings done in this way are called frescoes.

Paintings of the countryside were popular. They included pictures of wildlife and decorative panels of fruit.

Architectural scenes were also common. Some used tricks of perspective to make the room seem larger.

When the background was dry the details of the painting were added. For this stage the paints were mixed with egg-white to thicken them.

Paints were made from ground rocks, plant extracts or animal dyes.

Mosaics (pictures made of small pieces of tile or stone) were popular in Rome by the 1st century BC.

Figures from Greek mythology were often depicted.

Walls were also painted with portraits, possibly of the owner of the house. These are often very realistic.

Wet plaster was spread over a small area, then stones were pressed into it.

At first, regular patterns in black and white were most common. These remained fashionable around Rome.

Coloured stones were used to make detailed portraits, or patterns like the one shown here.

There were companies of mosaicists who designed the mosaic away from the house. Then someone came to the house with a plan, and the stones already cut.

Statues

Rooms were decorated with statues. They were brightly painted in Roman times, but the paint has now worn off.

Statues of sea creatures were sometimes built into fountains.

Gods and goddesses were common subjects.

Animals were also popular.

Food and dining

For breakfast most Romans ate bread or wheat biscuits with honey, dates or olives. They drank water or wine. The *prandium* (lunch) was a similar meal of bread, or leftovers from the previous day's main meal. However, instead of eating at lunchtime, many Romans waited until the main meal of the day, the *cena*. This was in the afternoon, after the daily visit to the baths.

During the early republic, the *cena* was very simple. The commonest food was wheat, often eaten as a kind of porridge, with sauces and vegetables. Meat was eaten only after animals had been sacrificed at religious festivals, or on special occasions. Later, however, meat became more common, and, for the wealthy, meals became more elaborate.

A dinner party

In rich imperial households, the *cena* was often very lavish. It was a way to entertain friends or important people, and hosts displayed their wealth by giving luxurious meals. This is how a banquet might have looked.

During the republic, only men could attend formal dinners. By imperial times, women often dined with the men. In early Rome people sat on chairs at tables. Later it was fashionable to dine lying on couches.

Romans did not use knives and forks. They mostly ate with their fingers, or sometimes with spoons. Slaves wiped the guests' hands between courses.

Some dining rooms were decorated with mosaics† showing scraps of food.

The fourth side of the table was left clear for slaves to bring food to the table and remove empty dishes.

The slaves also served wine with the meal. Sometimes it was heated in a warmer.

Poet waiting to read to the guests.

The menu

The dinner came in three courses. The first consisted of such appetizers as salad, radishes, mushrooms, oysters and other shellfish, sardines and eggs. This course was followed by a drink of *mulsum* (wine sweetened with honey).

The main course contained as many as seven dishes, including fish, meat and poultry. These were served with vegetables and sauces.

Rather than clearing the dishes after the main meal, the slaves removed the table and replaced it with another one, on which fruit, nuts and honey cakes were served. This part of the meal was called the *secundae mensae* (second tables).

The food was served with plenty of wine. The Romans had more than two hundred varieties from various parts of the empire. The best was said to come from Campania, near Naples.

Roman recipes

A recipe book from the fourth century AD, written by an expert on food called Apicius, gives us details of some Roman dishes and tells us how they were cooked.

Sauces were made with great care. The commonest, called *liquamen* or *garum*, was made from fish, salt and herbs. Some people made it themselves, but it was so popular that it could be bought ready-made.

Defrutum, another sauce, was obtained by boiling fruit juice until it reduced by a third. This was then added to other dishes.

Dining utensils

The food was brought into the dining room on serving dishes. Most of these were made of glass or pottery, but if the host was very rich there would also be ornately decorated platters made of gold and silver. Some examples are shown below.

Glass was made throughout the empire. It was often extremely ornate.

Silver drinking cup

Spoons

Silver strainer

Red, decorated pottery like this was popular all over the empire. It is known as Samian ware.

The Romans were highly skilled metalworkers. Intricately decorated serving dishes like this were often found in rich households.

The seating plan

Medius	3	2	1		3
					2
		1			1
Imus		2			
		3		Summus	

At formal banquets each couch seated three people. The couches were named *summus*, *medius* and *imus* (top, middle and bottom), and diners were seated according to their social status. The most honoured guest sat at *medius* 3, and the host often sat next to him at *imus* 1. A very rich host might have two tables of nine people each. Less formal dinners often had fewer than nine people.

The host also provided entertainment. Musicians, dancers, acrobats, conjurers and jugglers performed during the feast. At more elegant banquets the works of poets were read or sung.

Stuffed dates

For dessert Romans often ate stuffed dates. You can make these yourself.

Mash together some chopped apple and nuts, bread or cake crumbs, a pinch of cinnamon or nutmeg, and a little wine or fruit juice.

Cut the tops off the dates and remove the stones.

Push the filling in with a spoon.

Music and musicians

Though some rich citizens learned to play musical instruments they always remained amateurs, because they thought it was undignified to play, sing or dance in public. Professional musicians and dancers were usually slaves or freed men. As well as performing at dinner parties they also played in processions and parades, in the theatre and at the games. Here are some of the instruments they played.

Pipes   Lyre   Flute   Cymbals

Tambourine

In the kitchen

Most simple houses or apartments had no kitchens. The occupants could not cook in their living rooms because of the fire risk, so they had to visit a tavern whenever they wanted a hot meal. But rich people often had large, well-equipped kitchens in their houses. These were staffed by many slaves, each a specialist at preparing a particular type of food. They spent most of the day preparing the main meal. A typical Roman kitchen is shown below.

Pots like this, with pointed bottoms, were called *amphorae*. They were used for storing wine or oil.

Small *amphorae* were laid on shelves.

Large *amphorae* were propped up in the corner.

Food was cooked in earthenware or bronze pots on a stove full of hot charcoal.

Meat and poultry were roasted on spits over fires.

The cooks had sharp knives to chop vegetables.

To make sauces, ingredients had to be ground with a heavy pounder called a pestle, in a stone bowl called a mortar.

Kitchen utensils

Unlike the elaborate glass and metal utensils used for serving meals (see page 39), cooking pots were simply and strongly constructed to withstand a lot of use. Many utensils have been found at archaeological sites. Here are some examples.

Jugs were often made with very thick sides and only a small opening at the top, perhaps to keep water cool during hot weather.

This pottery strainer may have been used to drain liquid from curd cheese.

There were also pans that could be used for cooking or serving. This one also had a close-fitting lid.

Knives were beaten or cast out of metal, then sharpened. Some were given handles of wood, bone or ivory.

Metal sieves were used for straining wine or sauces. The holes in the bottom formed a decorative pattern.

Cooking pots were often placed on pottery or iron stands so that they did not rest directly on the fire.

This Roman relief shows slaves at work in a kitchen.

Two slaves are stoking the furnace.

A third is scooping flour from a sack.

Another is making dough or pastry.

Jewellery

At the beginning of the republic ornate jewels were rare. The law allowed only the upper classes to wear gold rings. However jewellery became more common after the Romans gained territories in the east, where precious metals were readily available. The materials most often used were gold, silver, bronze and iron, set with precious and semi-precious stones such as opals, emeralds and sapphires, and also with pearls. The Romans also polished glass and used it in place of precious stones. Both men and women wore rings. Women also wore a variety of earrings, necklaces, anklets, hairpins and brooches. In later imperial times these were very ornate. Pieces of jewellery have been found all over the Roman world. Here are some examples.

Gems often had designs cut into the surface, like this one found at Herculaneum.

Others were set into rings made from several pieces of gold.

A gold bracelet shaped like a snake was said to bring the wearer long life. These were found at Pompeii.

Fine gold chains were common. They were often made of many strands of metal, and worn as necklaces.

This bracelet is made from many strands of fine gold wire.

Each leaf in this necklace from Pompeii was stamped out of a sheet of gold.

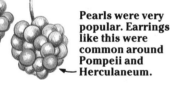

Pearls were very popular. Earrings like this were common around Pompeii and Herculaneum.

Earrings were mostly made of gold, sometimes with semi-precious stones attached. This pair, set with emeralds, was probably made around Naples.

Provincial jewellers used local materials. This bangle, found in England, was carved out of a stone called jet.

Pins such as these were made of ivory or gold and carved with various decorations. They were worn in the hair or pinned to clothing.

Cameos

Miniature carvings in semi-precious stone, known as cameos, were also popular. They were made from sardonyx, a rock with layers of different colours. Cameos were often worn as brooches or medallions.

The carver first chose his stone carefully to make sure that the colours would be clear and sharp after it was carved.

Then he cut the design so that the raised portion was a different colour from the base.

The most popular designs were pictures of the imperial eagle, or portraits of famous people.

This skeleton, found at Herculaneum, shows that Romans might have worn rings between the first and second joints of the finger, as well as below the second joint. Some people wore more than one ring on each finger.

Clothes and fashion

Roman paintings, statues and writings all provide information about clothes. Fashions in Rome changed very little for nearly a thousand years. Most people wore clothes made from wool or linen. In imperial times fine cotton cloth was imported from India, but was very expensive. Silk, from China, cost three times its weight in gold. Fur and felt were also used, especially in cold climates.

Most garments were made from large uncut pieces of cloth which were folded and pinned with pins called *fibulae*, or tied with belts. Garments needing a lot of sewing were rare, as most needles were made of bone and therefore very clumsy. Clothes were mainly the natural colours of their fibres, but some were bleached white or dyed various shades.

Men's clothes

A man's only underwear was a loincloth. He probably slept in one of these as well. Over this he wore a tunic, made from two rectangles stitched at the sides and shoulders, and tied with a belt. Augustus† is said to have worn four tunics at once when the weather was cold.

Loincloths were made of wool or linen.

Ordinary men wore tunics in various colours.

A senator's tunic had a purple stripe running down the front.

Outdoors, people in rural areas wore cloaks and trousers.

The toga

Originally only citizens† could wear the *toga*. Worn over the tunic, at first it was just a large woollen blanket wrapped round the body. Later it became more elaborate with complicated folds and drapes. Many people disliked the *toga* because it was heavy and awkward to wear, and hard to clean. But emperors tried to keep it in use because it was so distinctive. Like tunics, senators' *togas* were decorated with a purple stripe. *Togas* were sometimes worn in other shades, particularly black for funerals.

From statues and paintings it seems likely that the *toga* was folded from a semicircular piece of cloth 5.5m (18ft) long.

5.5m (18ft)

2.2m (7ft)

The rest of the right-hand piece was folded and thrown over the left shoulder.

A section of the left-hand straight edge was pulled up and tucked into the belt.

The left-hand end was thrown over the left shoulder.

A large fold was made from the middle of the right-hand section and gathered into a roll which was thrown over the left shoulder.

Women's clothes

As underwear women wore a loincloth and, sometimes, a brassière or corsets. Over this went a tunic, probably of fine wool or linen. On top of this was worn the *stola*, a robe which reached the ankles.

In early times women wore the *toga*, but later a garment called the *palla* became fashionable. It was a large rectangular piece of cloth which could be draped over the *stola* in many ways.

Tunic

Tunics were often made of plain, undyed cloth.

Richer women had brightly coloured *stolae* made of silk or fine Indian cotton.

Stola

Many women wore a veil or scarf to protect their hair when outside.

Palla

Some women wore the *palla* over their heads.

Children's clothes

Most boys and girls wore tunics like those of their parents. Some young boys wore the *toga praetexta*, a garment with a purple stripe. At about the age of 14 a special ceremony took place and they began wearing adult clothes (see page 48).

This mosaic shows children in tunics.

Bulla†   Toga praetexta

Stola

Some young girls wore the *stola*.

Men's hairstyles

During the early republic, many men wore beards, but from the 2nd century BC until the rule of Hadrian† it was the fashion in Rome to be cleanshaven. Most Roman men wore their hair short, but during imperial times some fashion-conscious men had longer hair which was oiled and curled. Some popular hairstyles are shown here.

Republican hairstyle

Later hairstyle

Early imperial hairstyles

The barber's shop was a place to meet friends and gossip. Being shaved was painful. Although the razor was sharp the barber used no oil or soap, so cuts and scars were frequent.

Women's hairstyles

Rich women spent a lot of time and money on their hairstyles, and had slaves to do their hair for them. Some of the most popular styles are shown here.

During the republic most women wore a simple bun.

Women sometimes cut the hair of blonde or red-headed slaves, and made it into wigs to wear themselves.

In imperial times hairstyles were very ornately plaited and curled.

Makeup

Women used various substances as makeup. They stored these in small pots and bottles.

It was fashionable to look as pale as possible. Women whitened their faces and arms with powdered chalk.

Eyelids were darkened with ash or a substance called antimony.

To colour their lips and cheeks red, they used the sediment from red wine, or a plant dye called *fucus*.

Pins

Heated tongs were used to curl hair, and pins made of bone or ivory were used to keep the hair in place.

Makeup pot

Hair-comb

Shoes

During the early republic, many Romans went barefoot most of the time, especially indoors. Outside they wore leather sandals. Later, footwear became more elaborate, and shoemakers became skilled at creating ornate sandals, shoes and boots out of canvas and leather.

Sandals were made out of leather.

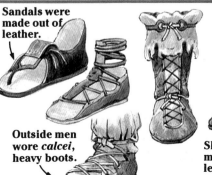

Outside men wore *calcei*, heavy boots.

Soldiers often wore boots that had soles studded with nails.

Slippers were made out of soft leather or cloth.

Women wore elegant sandals like these.

The Roman villa

The Romans used the word *villa* for a country house, as opposed to *domus* (town house; see page 34). Wealthy Romans saw the countryside as a source of income and as a place to rest from city life. Many villas were owned by rich city-dwellers who only spent part of the year in the country. At other times the estate was run by a manager and a team of slaves. Most villas were centres of farming (see overleaf). A few were supported by such other industries as pottery or mining. A very small number were lavish palaces that existed simply for their owners' pleasure.

An Italian villa

Most of the villas that have been excavated date from late imperial times. Few earlier villas remain, as their sites were often rebuilt or improved at a later period.

This reconstruction is based on remains found at various Italian sites. It shows a villa on an estate that made its money from farming and the production of olive oil and wine.

Decorations

The interiors of villas were often lavishly decorated. Mosaics (see page 37) were used to cover floors and walls. This one was found at a villa near Pompeii.

Triclinium (dining room)

Kitchen

The part where the owners from the city lived was very luxurious. It was called the *villa urbana*.

Paintings

The walls were also painted with colourful murals. Countryside scenes like this one were very popular.

A villa in the provinces

When the Romans conquered northern Europe, the population there consisted mostly of peasant farmers who lived in simple huts. The conquest opened up new opportunities for many of them. Gradually a new class of natives emerged – wealthy landowners who adopted Roman customs. They built large, important farmhouses based on Roman ones.

The pictures below show how this new style of farmhouse developed. They are based on details taken from excavations at a villa known as Lockleys, near St Albans, England.

One of the wings had two storeys.

▲ Before the conquest (c.AD50) the farmhouse was round with a thatched roof.

▲ Around AD60, after the conquest, it was rebuilt as a rectangular hut.

▲ About ten years later it was rebuilt and enlarged, with five rooms and a verandah.

Towards the end of the 2nd century the villa was redesigned. The new style is known as a winged-corridor villa, because the verandah was replaced by a corridor with an area known as a wing at each end. Later, in some villas, the wings were extended and linked with a wall, forming a courtyard inside.

The baths were here. They may have been used by both the owners and the workers.

There was a large area of farmland where vegetables were grown for the staff to eat.

Room where grapes were pressed.

This part of the villa was used by the farm staff. It was called the *villa rusticana*.

Cow shed

Grape juice was fermented in jars to make wine.

In the granary, the floor was raised on bricks to prevent damp reaching the grain.

Hadrian's villa

Hadrian† had a magnificent country villa at Tivoli, north-east of Rome. Its many buildings included a stadium, baths, libraries and a theatre. The surrounding gardens (shown here) occupied about 18 square km (7 square miles).

Ornaments

The gardens were decorated with fountains, and with statues of gods, people or animals. This statue of a child holding a fish formed the spout of an ornamental fountain.

Late provincial villas

By late in the 3rd century AD, villas in Britain were more lavish. Most mosaics that have been found date from this period. Though much of Roman Europe was under attack from barbarians†, Britain was quite a safe place to live. Some rich citizens† from more dangerous provinces may have sought refuge there. This is a reconstruction of a 3rd-century villa at Chedworth, Gloucestershire.

The Roman courtyard alone was bigger than the modern manor house that was later built on its grounds.

The foundations were built of chalk and flint.

The lower parts of the walls were made of flint and mortar.

45

Farming

Farming was one of the Romans' most important industries. Although basic farming methods changed little over the centuries, the Romans developed ways of making farms more efficient and productive. They introduced these ideas all over the empire and took better equipment to primitive countries like Britain. They also spread new crops, fruit and vegetables through the empire.

During the early republic most farms were very small, often worked by just one family and maybe one or two slaves†. These farmers grew enough to live on, and sold any surplus.

During the Punic† wars many farmers had to leave their farms to join the army. Their lands were neglected; some were devastated by battles and marching soldiers.

After the wars, many owners of small farms could not afford to repair the damage. Their land was bought by rich landowners and turned into large farms which were staffed by slaves.

An imperial farm

Many imperial farms produced a variety of goods, including crops, cattle, oil and wine, but some concentrated on just one or two of these products. The farm shown here has been reconstructed using details from Roman paintings, reliefs and mosaics, some of which are shown in the inset boxes.

Farmers kept as many as 200 chickens for their eggs and meat. Ducks and geese were also kept for their eggs, meat and feathers.

The ground had to be ploughed before seeds were planted. Seed was sown in autumn, and again in spring if needed.

Pigeons were kept in dovecotes and used as food in winter.

Grape press

Honey was the only form of sweetening available to Romans, so they kept bees.

Lettuces   **Carrots**

Cabbages

Radishes   **Beans**

Many farms were dedicated to growing food for the inhabitants of nearby towns. Market gardens were very prosperous, and we know from the remains of rubbish tips that the Romans had many different types of fruits and vegetables.

The most important working animal was the ox, which pulled ploughs and carts. The ones in this relief are pushing a threshing machine.

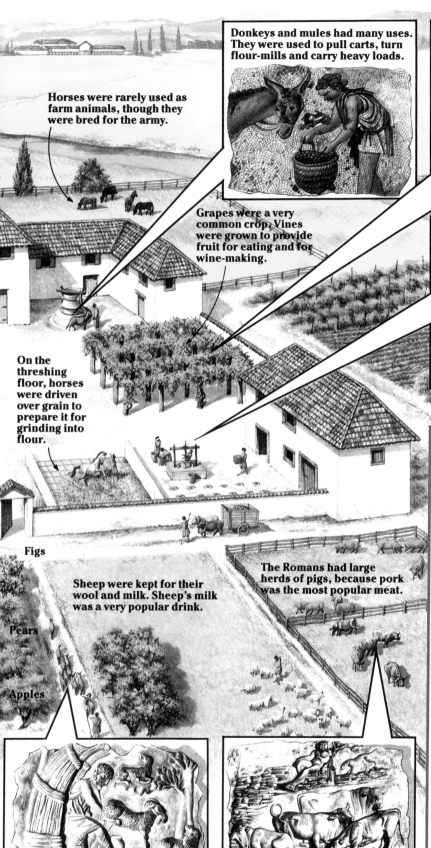

Donkeys and mules had many uses. They were used to pull carts, turn flour-mills and carry heavy loads.

When ripe, grapes were picked, put into a stone trough, and trodden to extract the juice. The juice was stored in jars to ferment into wine.

Horses were rarely used as farm animals, though they were bred for the army.

Grapes were a very common crop. Vines were grown to provide fruit for eating and for wine-making.

Olive trees grew all over Italy. Olive oil was used in cooking, as a form of soap, and as fuel for lamps. It was extracted from the olives in a special crusher like this.

On the threshing floor, horses were driven over grain to prepare it for grinding into flour.

Figs

Pears

Apples

Sheep were kept for their wool and milk. Sheep's milk was a very popular drink.

The Romans had large herds of pigs, because pork was the most popular meat.

Goats gave milk, and their hair was used to make rope and sacks. This relief shows a farmer milking a goat.

Cattle were also used for ploughing, and kept less often for milk or meat.

The rural ideal

Belief in the merits of rural life continued even among sophisticated imperial city-dwellers. This is partly why villas† were so popular with the urban rich. The countryside inspired Roman artists to create scenes like this, showing a rural goddess looking after a flock of sheep.

There were also many books about farming. Some, like Cato's *De Agri Cultura* (c.160BC), were manuals about how to run an estate. Others, however, like the *Georgics* by Virgil†, are lengthy poems in praise of rural life. But while city-dwellers idealized the country, the reality for farmers was often poverty, famine and disease.

47

Marriage and childbirth

Young Romans had little choice about whom they married. Parents chose husbands and wives for their children, and often arranged marriages for political, business or social reasons. Girls could marry at the age of 12, but most waited until they were at least 14. There were different types of marriage contract. In republican times a woman's money and possessions could become the property of her husband's father. Later, women controlled their own belongings and had more freedom.

The wedding day had to be carefully chosen because many days in the Roman calendar were thought to be unlucky. Weddings often took place in the second half of June, which was considered a particularly lucky period.

To celebrate an engagement, a party was held and the marriage contract was written out. The bride was given a ring for the third finger of her left hand. The night before the wedding, she offered her childhood toys to the gods at the household shrine.

On the wedding day, the bride's house was hung with flowers and ribbons. She wore a white tunic, a head-dress of flowers, and a red veil and shoes. Her hair was braided.

When the guests and bridegroom arrived the priest asked the gods if the day was a lucky one. If the answer was favourable the ceremony continued.

The contract was signed and the chief bridesmaid led the bride forward and joined her hand with the groom's. The couple prayed to the gods, and the bride promised to follow her husband wherever he went.

After the ceremony, there was a party at the house of the bride's father. Then the bride and groom led a procession of guests, flute players and torch-bearers to the groom's house. When they arrived, the groom carried the bride over the threshold.

Childbirth

Childbirth was very dangerous in Roman times. Medical science was primitive, and we know from tombstones that women often died giving birth. Children often died when they were still very small. Women married early partly because they believed that childbirth was safer when they were young. Some richer women, after giving birth to an heir, avoided having more children by using sponges as contraceptives.

A new baby was bathed and placed at its father's feet. The father picked up the child to show formally that he had accepted it into the family.

On the ninth day after the birth a ceremony took place at which the child was named. It was given a *bulla*, a charm to ward off evil spirits.

Becoming an adult

When a boy was about 14 years old, normally after he had finished his basic education, a ceremony was held at which he formally became an adult. With family and friends he went to the *forum*†, where he discarded his childhood clothes and *bulla*. He was given an adult's *toga*† and his first shave, and was registered as a citizen†. A party was held to celebrate.

Funerals and burial

When someone died, the Romans performed rituals based on their beliefs about what happened after death. Most people thought a dead person's spirit was rowed across a mythical river (the Styx), to the underworld (Hades†). The spirit was judged, then went to heaven (Elysium) or hell (Tartarus). Funerals prepared the dead person for the journey. A coin was placed under his or her tongue to pay the ferry fare to Hades. This is what happened after the death of a very important person.

The body lay in state in the *atrium*†, surrounded by lamps and candles.

When a nobleman died his body was washed and covered in oil.

Important citizens lay in state for several days, an emperor for a week. During this period people came to pay their respects.

If the man had held political office he was dressed in his official robes. Otherwise he wore a *toga*.

The body was covered in flowers and wreaths.

On the day of the funeral the body was placed on a portable bed known as a litter. Eight men carried the litter to the *forum* as part of a procession.

Praeficae (professional mourners) and torch-carriers followed the corpse.

Musicians

The procession stopped in the *forum*, where a speech was made in praise of the dead person.

In republican times relatives of the dead person rode in front of the procession. They wore death masks and mourning robes. This practice stopped in imperial times.

The body was taken to the grave; by law this had to be outside the city. Main roads were lined with magnificent tombs. The body was placed in a coffin made of stone or marble called a *sarcophagus*.

Sarcophagi were often intricately carved with scenes of daily life, hunts and battles.

The site of the grave was marked with a tomb, monument or mound of earth. Sometimes pillars or even high towers were built, such as this one at Igel in Germany, which is 23m (75ft) high.

Sometimes, instead of burying the body, the Romans cremated it. In simple ceremonies they dug a pit, filled it with wood, and burned the body. When the fire died down they covered the ashes with earth.

In more elaborate rituals the body was burned on a ceremonial fire known as a pyre. Relatives threw clothes and food into the flames, in case the dead person needed them later.

After the fire had died down it was doused with wine. The ashes were collected and placed in a jar called an urn. The urns were sometimes placed in a special underground chamber called a *columbarium*.

49

Education

Roman children were educated according to the wealth of their families. Many poorer children never learned to read or write because their parents needed them to work. Richer children started school when they were about six years old, attending a *ludus* (primary school). Most children left the *ludus* at the age of 11, and had any further education at home. But girls often began preparing for marriage, which could take place when they were 12 years old.

The school day

Most schools only had one room, on the ground floor of a house or behind a shop. There was usually only one class, of about 12 children. Remains of pupils' exercises, and descriptions by Roman writers of their education, tell us about the school day.

Teachers were often slaves brought back from Greece by the Roman army. The Romans respected the knowledge and learning of the Greeks.

Young children recited the alphabet and practised reading and writing.

Rich families employed a slave called a *paedagogus*, who took the children to school and supervised them while they were in class.

Older children had to learn and recite the works of famous authors.

Some pupils wrote on wooden tablets coated with wax.

Some pupils scratched their writing on bits of pottery.

The grammaticus

Around the age of 11 some boys went to a *grammaticus* (secondary school), where they learned such subjects as history, philosophy, geography, geometry, music and astronomy. One of the most important subjects was Greek, because Greek culture was such a big influence on Roman life. Works of Greek and Roman literature were studied in great detail. Pupils were expected to be able to imitate the styles of famous authors. Greek was also necessary for Romans because most of the best books on other subjects were written by Greeks.

Further education

One purpose of secondary education was to prepare the student for study with a teacher of public speaking called a *rhetor*. Anyone who wanted to be a politician or lawyer had to learn to speak in public. This training began when a youth was 13 or 14, and could take many years; Cicero† continued his studies until he was nearly 30. If parents were very rich they might send their sons to Athens or Rhodes to learn these skills from the best Greek teachers. Only the wealthiest people could afford to give their children this education, so few poor people became politicians or lawyers.

The *rhetor* taught his pupils how to write speeches properly and how to present them well.

Rhetor

Writing

In school, pupils practised writing by scratching on panels of wood coated with wax, using a pointed metal pen called a *stylus*. When the space on the tablet was used up, the wax was scraped off and more was applied. Some children scratched writing exercises on pieces of broken pottery. Older pupils were allowed to use pens made from reeds or metal. They wrote on sheets of papyrus (see below) with ink made of gum and soot.

Writing exercise on a piece of broken pottery.

Wax tablet

Reed pen →

Ink well

Stylus

Papyrus

In Roman times paper made from wood-pulp had not been invented. Instead the Romans used a material made from an Egyptian reed called papyrus. When papyrus was not available, parchment made from washed animal skin was used, but it was regarded as inferior to papyrus, probably because it was much heavier. The method of manufacturing papyrus is shown below.

A sheet was formed of two layers of strips, placed at right angles to each other and pressed together. The starch from the core acted as a sort of glue.

To prepare papyrus for writing, the outer rind of the reed was removed and the core was cut into long, narrow strips and soaked.

The sheet was beaten with a mallet, left to dry, then polished with a stone.

The sheets were then glued together side by side to form a longer one. When this was dry it was rolled up into a scroll.

Sometimes rollers of wood or ivory were fitted at each end of the scroll. This made it easier to handle.

The joins between the sheets could hardly be seen in well-made scrolls.

Books

The Romans were very fond of books. In large cities like Rome and Alexandria there were numerous bookshops and publishers. Many people treasured books, and built up large collections of them. The state, and also some rich individuals, set up libraries for the public to use.

By the late Empire there were 29 libraries in Rome. Books took a long time to make, because each one had to be written out by hand. They were copied by scribes who were often Greek slaves. This picture shows how a manuscript was copied.

The text was written in columns. When one column was finished the scribe began another one to the right.

Publishers employed a man to read the book to a team of scribes. Each scribe wrote a copy of the book.

The scribe sat with the ends of the scroll to his right and left, and wrote on the side of the scroll on which the fibres lay horizontally.

Rolls varied in length, but were commonly around 10m (30ft). Many were beautifully illustrated. Some had parchment covers.

The rolls were often stored in a leather casket.

The codex

In the 4th century AD the scroll began to be replaced by the *codex*, in which the pages were secured at one side. The *codex* was adopted by the Christian † Church because it held more information than a scroll, and was easier to store, carry and read.

Jobs and occupations

Upper-class Romans did not respect physical labour, and would consider only a few careers, such as the army, politics, or some forms of financial work. Skilled jobs like architecture (see pages 70-73) or medicine (see pages 68-69) were done by educated members of the middle class, foreigners, or freed men (see opposite). Most poorer citizens† worked as craftsmen or shopkeepers; those in rural areas owned or worked on farms (see pages 46-47). Manual labour like building or mining was done almost entirely by slaves (see opposite).

Most craftsmen worked in small workshops, with a few apprentices and perhaps one or two slaves. They worked at the back of the shop, and sold their goods in the front. Other shopkeepers bought their goods from wholesale markets and then sold them to the public from their shops. A typical Roman street might have contained some of the shops shown here.

Meat, produced from specially bred cattle, was sold wholesale to butchers at a market called the *forum boarium*. The butcher then sold to the public. Some butchers sold poultry as well.

Carpenters made furniture or worked in the building trade. The workshop was equipped with many types of tool still in use today.

Potters designed and made crockery of all kinds. They cast the pots on wheels and baked them in kilns over wooden fires.

Bakers ground flour and baked bread at the back of their shops, then sold it over a counter at the front. The loaves were given distinctive patterns.

Metalworkers made tools, weapons, and household goods, most commonly out of bronze, iron and copper. Jewellers made brooches, rings and ornmaments out of gold, silver and precious stones (see page 41).

Working women

The lives of Roman women depended on how rich they were. Rich families thought it inappropriate for women to go out to work. Instead wealthy women directed the work of slaves and organized the running of the home. They were also expected to have babies, and slaves helped them to bring up their children. We know that a few women became doctors or teachers, but these were rare.

In ordinary families women had to spin and weave woollen cloth to make clothes. All women were taught these skills, but most rich families bought ready-made cloth.

Poorer women worked in markets, as needlewomen, or as attendants at the baths. Some served in shops, like the one shown in this relief.

In the country, women worked on farms and as shepherdesses. A farmer's wife worked on the estate with her husband.

Slaves and slavery

Slaves were workers with no rights or status who were owned by Roman citizens, or by the state. They were bought and sold like any other property, and their lives were controlled by their owners. Like other ancient peoples, the Romans thought this situation was quite natural. There were very few slaves during the early republic, but after the 3rd century BC the number grew as Rome conquered other countries. After each new victory prisoners of war were brought back to Rome. They were exhibited at markets with signs round their necks advertising their qualities.

Slaves were sold by auction to the highest bidder.

A slave's life

In imperial times there was a vast workforce of slaves. Their lives varied depending on the jobs they did and whom they worked for. The law allowed slave-owners to treat their slaves however they wished. Many slaves suffered terribly at the hands of cruel masters, but others lived well. Here are some of the jobs that slaves did.

Greek slaves were thought to be the cleverest, so they were the most expensive. They worked in richer Roman houses as doctors, tutors, musicians, goldsmiths, artists and librarians. Other slaves worked as hairdressers, butlers, maids and cooks. Some helped their owners in shops or factories.

Slaves owned by good masters in the country often lived better than poor citizens in towns. They worked in pleasant surroundings, and could marry and have children. Many also ran small farms of their own.

The government itself owned many slaves, who maintained buildings, bridges and aqueducts. Others worked as civil servants, helping the administration of the empire. Some became very powerful and important.

Slaves who worked in mines suffered particularly bad conditions. They were harshly treated and forced to work constantly in mines that were often unsafe. Many died as a result of injuries or beating.

There were several rebellions by discontented slaves. The most famous was led by Spartacus, who formed an army of slaves in 73BC. It had up to 90,000 members until it was defeated by the Roman army two years later.

Some slaves were paid wages. If they saved enough, they could pay their masters to set them free. Others did not have to pay, as some owners freed their favourite slaves as a reward. By imperial times freed men were a large, rich sector of the population. Many became businessmen, and were a vital part of the economy. Others became important administrators or civil servants (see page 27).

At the freedom ceremony the slave wore a special cap and was given a *toga praetexta* †.

53

Money and trade

The Roman economic system changed as the empire grew. During the early republic money was not used; people simply exchanged one kind of goods for another (this is known as bartering). Later, economic transactions were conducted using blocks of bronze weighing one Roman pound (327g/11.44oz). But as the Romans gained territory, they became richer and the economy became more complex. Coins were introduced, and trade and taxation reorganized. By imperial times an intricate economic system co-ordinated money and trade all over the Roman world.

Republican coins

Coins were first widely used by the Greeks. After seeing Greek coins in central Italy, the Romans opened their first mint around 290BC. Soon there were several Roman mints, all producing their own coins. The names and styles changed often, and, as prices kept rising, so did the values.

The first Roman coin, the *as*, was ▶ bronze. Asses had the heads of gods or goddesses on one side and pictures of ships on the other.

Around 269BC the first silver ▶ coin, the *didrachm*, was introduced. This one shows Mars, the god of war.

◀ Later a silver coin called the *denarius* was issued. This one shows a man voting in the elections. There were at first 10, and later 16 asses to a *denarius*.

Another silver coin, the ▶ *sestertius*, was first worth 2.5 asses, later 4.

The *aureus*, Rome's first gold coin, was introduced during the second Punic† war.

◀ Coins were used to mark important events. This one from about 42BC shows Brutus† on one side. The other shows a cap and a pair of daggers. 'EID MAR' means 'The Ides of March', the date of Caesar's assassination.

Early imperial coins

When Augustus became emperor he took control of the mints, and all gold and silver coins were made under his supervision. But mints in the provinces were allowed to produce their own bronze and copper coins, because they were less valuable. Augustus standardized the monetary system and gave all coins a fixed value. They were used all over the empire, and this encouraged trade (see opposite).

Every coin had the emperor's head on it ▶ to prove it was genuine. The largest gold coin, still called the *aureus*, was roughly 8 grams (¼oz) of gold.

The silver *denarius* ▶ now weighed about 4 grams (⅛oz). An *aureus* was worth 25 *denarii*.

During the Empire the *sestertius* was minted in bronze, not silver; ◀ there were 4 *sestertii* in a *denarius*.

A *dupondius* was ◀ worth half a *sestertius*.

The *as* was made ▶ of copper. There were 4 to a *sestertius*.

There were 2 ◀ bronze *semis* to an *as*.

There were 4 copper *quadrans* ▶ in an *as*.

Later imperial coins

Prices rose constantly, so people could buy less and less with their coins. New ones of higher values had to be minted. But the cost of precious metals increased too, so mints were forced to reduce the weight of coins, or to make them in copper with only a thin coating of precious metal.

This type of coin, known as the *solidus*, was first issued by Constantine†. He intended it to become the standard coin, as it was difficult to forge and everyone knew what it was worth. The *solidus* was made from about 5g (⅙oz) of gold.

Towards the end of the Empire people became suspicious of money because prices rose so quickly, coins contained less precious metal and forgeries were common. Many Romans abandoned coins and returned to bartering.

Banking

After the Punic† wars, the Romans controlled a huge trading network. Merchants and businessmen needed money to finance trading projects, so money-lending and banking became important parts of the economy. These services were provided mainly by *equites†* and freed men†, as patricians† thought financial work was undignified. Many members of the middle classes became very rich.

This relief shows a banker at his desk. There were moneychangers and bankers all over the empire. Some were controlled by the government, but others operated individually.

Many people found themselves unable to repay their debts. When this happened they had their property confiscated. Some were even sold into slavery.

Taxes

The government imposed taxes to raise money to run the state. Taxation changed from time to time, and differed in each area. Some of the main types of tax are described below.

Provincials†, and later Roman citizens† themselves, paid tax on their property, houses, farms, slaves and animals. Travelling inspectors assessed how much tax people had to pay.

Some financial transactions were subject to tax, including buying and selling property or slaves. People also paid tax on money they inherited. This stone relief shows people paying a tax collector.

There was no centrally organized system of distributing food to soldiers. Instead farmers had to reserve a portion of their grain and other goods for any troops based on their land.

Trade

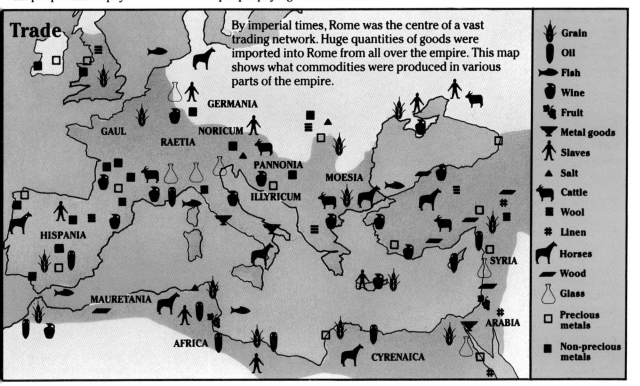

By imperial times, Rome was the centre of a vast trading network. Huge quantities of goods were imported into Rome from all over the empire. This map shows what commodities were produced in various parts of the empire.

GERMANIA
GAUL
RAETIA
NORICUM
PANNONIA
ILLYRICUM
MOESIA
HISPANIA
MAURETANIA
AFRICA
CYRENAICA
SYRIA
ARABIA

Grain
Oil
Fish
Wine
Fruit
Metal goods
Slaves
Salt
Cattle
Wool
Linen
Horses
Wood
Glass
Precious metals
Non-precious metals

Entertainments

Many Roman citizens had a lot of free time, as slaves† did most of their work. Evidence of Roman leisure activities comes from archaeological finds, mosaics and paintings, and the writings of Roman authors. Some popular amusements are described here and on the next five pages.

Pastimes

Public gardens and parks were popular places to relax and chat. Romans also enjoyed many forms of exercise, including running, javelin throwing and wrestling. For these activities there were exercise grounds like the Campus Martius in Rome. There was also space for less energetic activities like the ones described below.

People scratched criss-cross patterns on the ground to play games like draughts with counters like these.

Gambling games with coins included *capita et navia*, the Roman equivalent of heads and tails.

Tali (knucklebones) was played with pieces of bone or pottery. The pieces had numbers on the sides and were thrown like dice.

Rich men were fond of hunting and fishing. They wore the special costumes shown in this mosaic.

We know from the writings of Horace† that children built toy houses, used whips and tops, kites and hoops, and played on see-saws and swings. Reliefs, paintings and mosaics show pictures of the games that children played. Many of their pastimes imitated the activities of adults.

Dolls like this were moulded from clay, then carved and painted.

Rag dolls and jointed dolls made of wood were also common.

Sometimes children rode in carts pulled by geese, as shown in this mosaic.

The theatre

The theatre became popular in Rome during the 3rd century BC after the Romans came into contact with the Greeks. At first plays were staged in primitive wooden theatres, but in 55BC the first stone theatre was built in Rome by Pompey†. It held up to 27,000 people. Stone theatres were later built all over the empire. The remains of these show us what the inside of a theatre might have looked like.

Each part of the auditorium was reserved for a different class of people. The poorer they were, the higher up they sat.

In early days the public stood to watch the play. Later theatres were built with stone seats.

People brought cushions to make the seats more comfortable.

People could leave the theatre very quickly because there was an intricate network of corridors and stairs.

To keep the sun off the spectators, canvas covers were spread over the auditorium, stretched from poles at the back of the top row of seats.

Roman actors wore masks on stage. This was because most Roman plays included the same types of characters, and the masks made them easier to identify from a distance.

Scenery and backcloths were sometimes hung behind the actors.

The scenery was manipulated by complicated machinery, and was often very elaborate and realistic.

Scene changes were hidden by a curtain which was lifted from a slot at the front of the stage.

The actors appeared on the *pulpitum* (stage).

At first only men were allowed on stage. Later, women performed too.

Some benches were also arranged in front of the stage with the best seats reserved for senators.

The audience was rowdy, clapping, booing, hissing and often fighting. Some actors were so popular that they were mobbed by their fans.

Plays and writers

The first play was shown in Rome in 240BC. It was a Greek drama, translated into Latin by a Greek former slave called Livius Andronicus. Though serious plays were popular at first, audiences began to want comedies. The most famous Roman comic writers were Plautus† and Terence†. This wall-painting at Pompeii shows a scene from a play by Plautus.

Gradually theatrical shows became more spectacular, to compete with races and public games (see pages 60-61). Eventually people went to the theatre more for the special effects than the plays themselves.

Races and games

Public entertainments in Rome were called *ludi* (games). Many were paid for by the government as they were part of the religious calendar (see pages 66-67). There were three kinds of entertainment: theatrical performances (*ludi scaenici*, see page 56), chariot races (*ludi circenses*), and gladiator fights and beast hunts (*munera*). At first these events were staged together to form a whole day's entertainment. By imperial times, however, each event could be seen separately, often in its own specially designed building.

Chariot races

Chariot racing was the most popular spectator sport in Rome. Races were held at a racecourse called the circus or hippodrome. As many as 24 races took place in a day, with up to 12 chariots from four different teams. This is what a chariot race would have looked like.

The races were directed by an important person (sometimes the emperor himself) who started each race by throwing a white cloth from his raised platform.

A central rib, the *spina*, ran down the centre of the course, with three pillars at each end.

Each race usually lasted for seven laps. These were counted by removing objects shaped like dolphins or large eggs from racks on the *spina*.

The four different teams were identified by the colours red, green, blue and white.

The drivers jostled for a position close to the *spina*. This was to secure the shortest route round the bend, the most dangerous part of the race.

The driver wound the reins around his body, and carried a knife to cut through them if he was thrown from the chariot.

The *Circus Maximus* in Rome, shown here, was the largest and oldest racetrack in the empire. It was 550m (over 1800ft) long and 180m (almost 600ft) wide, and held up to 250,000 spectators.

Usually either two or four horses pulled each chariot, but sometimes special races were held with six or even eight horses to a team. The more horses, the harder it was to control the chariot.

Each team had its own stables and trainers. Supporters of the teams were fanatical, and unpopular results could lead to riots. Champion drivers, like the one in this mosaic†, became very rich and famous.

Gladiator fights

Gladiators were prisoners, criminals, slaves, or paid volunteers, who fought for the public's entertainment. Gladiator fights and shows involving wild animals were very popular in Rome. At first, like chariot races, they were held in the circus, but later they were staged in stone buildings called amphitheatres†. Games were often put on by individuals to mark an important event like a battle victory. The earliest games were small, but they gradually became more extravagant. Trajan† presided over a show that lasted 117 days in which 10,000 gladiators took part.

There were amphitheatres all over the empire. The largest held up to 50,000 spectators. Rich citizens sat in the best seats, near ground level. Poorer people sat higher up.

Games began in the morning with a procession past the seat of the emperor or presiding official. The gladiators were accompanied by dancers, jugglers, priests and musicians.

Next came the beast shows. Some rare animals were simply displayed. More common animals, like bears, panthers and bulls were forced to fight each other, hunted in the arena by archers, or let loose on defenceless prisoners. Many fights involved the bloody and violent killing of thousands of animals and humans. After the beasts came comic acts, mimes and mock fights.

Vats of incense were used to disguise the smell of the blood.

Retiarius

Murmillo

Samnite

Thracian

The sand was often coloured so that the blood did not show up so much.

The gladiators fought in the afternoon. There were four types, distinguished by their weapons and costumes. To make the show more interesting, gladiators in different categories fought each other; for example a *retiarius* might fight a *murmillo*. They normally continued to the death, but defeated or wounded fighters could appeal for mercy. After listening to the crowd, the official in charge signalled with his thumb whether the man should live or die. We think that the 'thumbs up' signal meant that the gladiator should live, but we have nothing to prove this.

A successful gladiator received money, a crown, and great adulation. After many victories he might be awarded a wooden sword, which signified his freedom. Many freed fighters became trainers at special schools for gladiators.

59

The baths

The first bath-houses, built in the 2nd century BC, were simple washing facilities for men only. But by the time of Augustus† there were 170 privately owned bath-houses, and in AD20 the first large state-owned public baths were opened. Baths grew in size and splendour in imperial times; they became huge centres where thousands of people spent their leisure hours. We know from the ruins of baths that they were sophisticated buildings with complicated heating and plumbing systems. This is what a Roman bath-house might have looked like.

Libraries and reading rooms were also common in the larger baths.

Emperors had baths built to show off their power and wealth. The buildings were often extremely lavish, full of gold and marble. In imperial times it only cost a *quadrans* (the smallest Roman coin) to get in. The baths were open from dawn until sunset.

The *frigidarium* was a room with a large cold swimming pool.

Clothes were left in the *apodyterium* (cloakroom), but thefts were common.

There was an exercise yard for wrestling, training, and various kinds of sport.

Rich people took their slaves to the baths to help them and look after the clothes.

Baths were often built in places where the water was thought to have medicinal properties. People visited them in the hope that the waters would cure their illnesses.

Various snacks were sold for the bathers to eat.

Some baths also had shops and restaurants, either actually in the complex itself or close by.

Sometimes there was an outdoor pool.

There were several types of bath at different temperatures.

A huge wood-fired hypocaust system (see page 34) conducted heat under the floors and into the room.

The hottest room of all, the *laconicum*, was used mainly by invalids. A tub of boiling water in the centre kept it steamy.

The hot room, the *caldarium*, had a pool for bathing. In this damp atmosphere people sweated a lot.

After bathing, customers could hire attendants for a massage. Barbers and hairdressers were also available, as were beauty treatments.

The *tepidarium* was a warm room with a small pool.

Keeping clean

The Romans did not have soap. To remove dirt and sweat they covered their bodies with oil which they then scraped off with strigils (scrapers made of wood, bone or metal).

People played games of knucklebones (see page 56), dice or chequers.

Famous baths

By AD284 there were around 1000 private bath-houses and 11 public ones. Among the most impressive in Rome were those opened by the emperors Caracalla and Diocletian. This is a reconstruction of the Baths of Caracalla.

There were gardens where people could stroll before or after their baths. They were a good place to socialize and catch up with all the latest gossip.

Religious beliefs

The Romans had many different gods and goddesses. They fell into two main groups: spirits that were thought to protect houses and were worshipped domestically, and the gods and goddesses of the formal state religion who were worshipped at public ceremonies. Worship of household spirits was the earliest form of Roman religion; the rituals of the organized state religion (see below) became more elaborate during the expansion of the empire.

Worship at home

Romans believed that their homes were controlled by groups of *numina* (household spirits). One group, the *penates*, protected the stores; another, the *lares*, looked after the whole household. Each family also had its own guardian spirit, the *genius*, and ancestral spirits, the *manes*. These beliefs began among early farmers, but were retained in the sophisticated urban houses of imperial Rome. Some *numina* took on individual personalities and names. These included Vesta, goddess of the hearth, and Janus, god of the doorway.

Each house had a shrine to the *lares* called a *lararium*, where the family prayed each day, and offered small gifts such as wine, bread or fruit.

The growth of religion

As the Romans conquered areas outside Rome itself they met people who worshipped other gods and goddesses. Rather than suppressing these other religions, they often adopted them. As the empire expanded the number of deities grew.

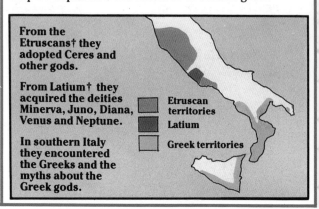

From the Etruscans† they adopted Ceres and other gods.

From Latium† they acquired the deities Minerva, Juno, Diana, Venus and Neptune.

In southern Italy they encountered the Greeks and the myths about the Greek gods.

Etruscan territories

Latium

Greek territories

The state religion

The Romans were attracted to Greek mythology. They matched their Roman gods (see overleaf) with the Greek ones, making them the basis of their state religion. This required worshippers to observe strict rituals at elaborate ceremonies. Romans could worship any number of gods, and did this by praying and making sacrifices. Most people believed that they were protected by a particular god or goddess. They also believed that each deity looked after a particular aspect of life. For example, people prayed to Venus for success in love, or to Mars for success in war.

Temples and ceremonies

The state deities had large and impressive temples built for them. Their layout was adopted from those of the Etruscans and Greeks. Temples contained treasure that had been won in battle or had been donated by individuals as a way of thanking the gods for help. People were also allowed to store their own gold in the temple, which was looked after by priests and priestesses.

On public holidays and festivals (see pages 66-67) a long procession of priests, government officials and musicians approached the temple, leading animals which were to be sacrificed.

The temple housed the statue of the god.

Ceremonies were held outside the temple, but individuals could go inside to say private prayers.

Making sacrifices

Animals were sacrificed at an altar in front of the temple. Only priests could conduct the ceremony because it was very complex. If any detail of the ritual went wrong, the Romans believed the gods would not accept the sacrifice. Priests were therefore very important. The chief priest was called the *Pontifex Maximus*. From the time of Augustus† this position was held by the emperor himself.

Citizens† wishing to make offerings brought beasts to the temple. The animals most frequently used were oxen, sheep, pigs, goats and doves.

The priest washed his hands, called for silence, and sprinkled salt, flour or wine on the animal's head. When he signalled that all was ready, attendants carried out the sacrifice.

Parts of the animal's carcass were thrown onto the altar fire for the god to consume.

Foretelling the future

The Romans believed strongly in supernatural forces. They had many ways of predicting the future and learning the will of the gods. People performed all kinds of rites to ensure their safety and wellbeing, and consulted various fortune tellers. Some of these are shown below.

Haruspices were special priests who examined the innards of sacrificed animals. It was thought that the shape of an animal's liver, and the presence or absence of blemishes on it, would reveal the attitude of the gods towards public projects and government policies.

In Rome there was a group of 16 prophets called augurs. They examined the sky for flocks of birds, cloud shapes, lightning, and other natural events. They believed that these things were omens that could tell them the opinions of the gods.

In times of national crisis, the Romans consulted books of prophecies written by the Sibyl†, a prophetess who lived in caves at Cumae in early republican times. The books were closely guarded in Rome, and contained advice about how to interpret the will of the gods.

Astrologers told fortunes by examining the position of the stars at the time of a person's birth. By imperial times the practice was very widespread. Even emperors consulted astrologers, to try to protect themselves from assassination.

Poorer people had ways of foretelling the future, including palm reading and throwing special dice.

People also thought that illness could be cured by miracles or by treatments suggested in dreams. To have such dreams the patient slept in the temple of Aesculapius, the god of medicine (see page 69).

Gods and goddesses

This family tree shows the most important gods of the state religion (see page 62) and their spheres of influence. Each Roman name is followed by its Greek equivalent in brackets.

Uranus ══ Gaea

Cronus ══ Rhea

Vesta (Hestia), goddess of the hearth.

Ceres (Demeter) goddess of agriculture.

Juno (Hera), wife ══ and sister of Jupiter, goddess of women and childbirth.

Jupiter (Zeus), king of the gods, and god of thunder and lightning.

Neptune (Poseidon), god of the sea.

Dis (Pluto), god of the underworld.

Vulcan (Hephaestus), god of craftsmen and forges.

Mars (Ares), god of war.

Diana (Artemis), goddess of the moon and hunting.

Minerva (Athena), goddess of crafts and war.

Mercury (Hermes), god of trade and thieves, Jupiter's messenger.

Bacchus (Dionysus), god of wine.

Venus (Aphrodite), daughter of Uranus and Gaea, goddess of love and beauty.

Apollo, god of the sun, music, healing and prophecy. (The Romans adopted Apollo from the Greeks; he had no Roman equivalent.)

══ This symbol means 'married'.

The vestal virgins

Vesta was a household deity before becoming a state goddess. She had a shrine in the *forum*, where a fire burned constantly. It was tended by six women called Vestal Virgins, who are shown in this relief. They were chosen from Rome's leading families. It was an honour to be selected, but they had to do the job for 30 years and were not allowed to marry.

Other deities

There were many other lesser gods. Some, like Flora, Faunus, Pomona and Silvanus, were responsible for growth and fertility. There were also several gods and goddesses of war, including Quirinus and Bellona. The god of love was Cupid. Roma was the goddess of Rome itself.

Flora

Cupid

Quirinus

Roma

Alternatives to the state religion

Many Romans lost faith in the state religion, as it offered little more than rituals and did not satisfy their personal needs. Also, when affairs of state went badly people found it increasingly hard to believe that sacrifices and prayers had any effect. By the start of the Empire many Romans had abandoned the state religion. Augustus† tried with some success to restore it, but people wanted other religious experiences and turned to the various cults that reached Rome from other countries as the empire grew. These required people to take part in ceremonies rather than just watch them. Some promised life after death and offered more personal involvement than the state religion could. Here are some of the gods, goddesses and religions that the Romans adopted.

◄ Epona, the Celtic goddess of horses, was first worshipped in Gaul. But her cult was spread, probably by Gaulish soldiers, to Spain, Germany, the Danube, Scotland, and into Italy itself.

Cybele, an important foreign goddess, ▶ was also known as the Great Mother. She ruled fertility, healing and nature, and was very popular with women. Her cult was brought to Rome from Asia Minor in 204BC, when a prophet warned that the Romans would lose the Carthaginian wars without Cybele's help. The ceremonies included wild music and dancing, processions and sacrifices. This made some Romans suspicious of the cult, but Claudius† gave it public status.

Mithras

◄ Worship of the god Mithras began in India and Persia. Mithraism became popular all over the Roman world, especially among soldiers. It offered life after death, and asked people to treat others with kindness and respect. The religion stated that all men were equally worthy, whether senators or slaves, but women were not allowed to join the cult. Mithraic temples have been found throughout the empire.

Cybele

Judaism was an ancient religion that the ▶ Romans encountered when they conquered Palestine in 63BC and made it the province† of Judaea. Many Romans turned to Judaism instead of the state religion, and at first it was officially tolerated. But later Jews were badly persecuted because they believed in only one god and refused to worship the emperor as the state demanded. There were many revolts against Roman rule, and in AD70 the Romans destroyed the Jewish temple at Jerusalem. This event is depicted on the arch of Titus.

◄ The cult of Isis began in Egypt and later spread all over the empire. Isis was the ruler of heaven and earth, and goddess of wheat and barley. The cult became fashionable when the Egyptian queen Cleopatra spent the year 45BC in Rome. Isis was associated with goodness and the purification of sin. The Romans were attracted to the cult because it was so ancient. Ceremonies were very elaborate and mysterious.

This early Christian wall-painting shows Jesus as a shepherd.

◄ Christianity was founded in Palestine by the followers of Jesus of Nazareth (c.5BC-AD29), and spread rapidly through the empire. It was particularly popular with the poor, who found comfort in its promise of everlasting life. Like Jews, Christians believed there was only one god, and refused to worship the state gods. This angered the Roman government. Christians had to meet in secret, and were often harshly persecuted. But the religion continued to grow, and in AD313 official toleration of Christianity was declared by Constantine (see page 77). It became the official state religion in AD394.

Phoenician gods

Baal

Baal and Tanit were ancient Phoenician gods that the Romans encountered in Carthage. At first the rituals of their cult included human sacrifices, but these were forbidden after the Romans conquered Carthage in 146BC. The cult survived in parts of Spain and North Africa into the 1st century AD.

A shrine to another Carthaginian god, Melkart, was founded in 1100BC at Cadiz in Spain. By 400BC the Romans had linked Melkart to the god Hercules (himself derived from the Greek god Heracles). The cult continued into the 5th century AD.

When the Romans conquered ▶ new areas they took their gods with them. Locals were not forced to adopt Roman gods, but they were often curious about them. Native deities were merged with Roman ones, so local versions of the state gods emerged all over the empire. This temple at Trier in Germany was built for Mars Lenus, a god of healing.

Festivals

The Romans had many festivals, each with its own social or religious significance. They were often public holidays, although business was forbidden on only the most solemn occasions. During the rule of Augustus† there were at least 115 holidays each year. Under some later emperors there were more than 200 festival days a year. Many festivals were celebrated with games, races and theatrical performances (see pages 56-59). Below is a calendar of some of the most important events. The reason for the celebration is given, and, where known, the festival's Latin name.

1 January

New consuls† were sworn in. Bulls were sacrificed to Jupiter as thanks for his protection in the past year. The consuls promised that their successors would do the same the following year.

Early January — Compitalia

In the country, each farmer built a small shrine with an altar at the boundary of his farm. He placed a plough there and a wooden doll for each person in his household. The next day was a holiday. A sacrifice was made to purify the farm for the coming year.

In the city, the president of each *insula*† sacrificed a hen on an altar built at each crossroads. Three days of celebrations followed.

13-21 February — Parentalia

Parentalia was a ceremony to honour dead parents. Romans visited the cemeteries outside the city where they placed flowers, milk and wine on the graves of their parents. This was to stop the dead feeling hungry and returning to plague the living.

15 February — Lupercalia

Two teams of youths met at the Lupercal, a cave on the Palatine, and raced round the hill. Crowds gathered to watch. The runners dressed in the skins of sacrificed goats and were smeared with blood. As they ran they whipped the spectators with strips of goatskin. This was said to promote fertility, so women wanting children stood close to the race.

22 February — Caristia

This was a ceremony to conclude the *Parentalia*. It was an occasion on which families gathered together for a joyful dinner.

1 March

A ritual took place in the temple of Vesta at which the perpetual fire was re-kindled. This day was also the beginning of the dances of the *Salii* (college of priests). Twelve young patricians† danced around Rome holding sacred shields. This continued for 19 days. The dancers feasted at a different house each night.

14 March

Horse races were held in the *Campus Martius* † to mark the feast of Mars, the god of War.

15 March

This was a festival for Anna Perenna, goddess of the year. People took picnics to the River Tiber. Some Romans believed that they would live as many years as they could drink cups of wine.

23 March — Tubilustrium

On this day sacred trumpets of war were purified at a ceremony to the god Mars. This was to bring success in the coming battle season.

4-10 April — Ludi Megalenses

Games were held to honour Cybele, the Great Mother (see page 65).

12-19 April — Ludi Ceriales

Games were held to honour Ceres, goddess of corn.

21 April — Parilia

Parilia began as a country festival to purify sheep and keep disease from the flock. But later it was celebrated in Rome itself because the date was said to have been the birth of the city. Each area of Rome organised its own festivities. These included bonfires onto which offerings were thrown. People danced in the flames. *Parilia* ended with a large outdoor feast.

28 April-May 3 — Ludi Florales

This was a carnival in honour of Flora, the goddess of flowers, and a celebration of fertility. It was also known as *Floralia*. People danced wearing brightly coloured garlands. Tables were piled high with flowers.

9 June — Vestalia

Married women went to the temple of Vesta with gifts of food for the goddess. *Vestalia* was a holiday for bakers, because the Vestal Virgins produced loaves made from *mola salsa*, a salted flour.

24 June — Fors Fortuna

This was the festival for the goddess Fortuna. There was a great public holiday. People rowed down the River Tiber to watch sacrifices at the two shrines to Fortuna, just outside Rome. The rest of the day was spent picnicking and drinking.

6-13 July — Ludi Apollinares

During the republic this festival was connected with religious ceremonies to the god Apollo. But by imperial times it was simply an excuse for theatrical shows, games and races.

12 August

The god Mercury was known for his sly practices and cunning. He was particularly popular among businessmen and traders, who paid 10% of their profits to his shrine. The money was used to pay for a public feast which took place on this day.

13 August

This day was a feast to Diana. Slaves had a holiday. It was also traditional for women to wash their hair.

5-19 September — Ludi Romani

At first this 15-day festival of games, races and theatre was to honour Jupiter, but later much of the religious significance disappeared. On 13 September a cow was sacrificed at Jupiter's temple, and the Senate and all the magistrates ate a banquet there. Statues of Jupiter, Juno and Minerva were dressed up and placed on couches so that they could share the feast with the humans.

4-17 November — Ludi Plebeii

Theatre, games and races marked this feast to Jupiter. On 13 November there was a banquet for senators and magistrates.

Early December — Rites of the Bona Dea

This festival was in honour of the Bona Dea ('Good Goddess'), whom the Romans believed protected women. The rituals were secret, and men were strictly forbidden to attend. The rites may have involved dancing, drinking and the worship of sacred objects.

17 December — Saturnalia

At first *Saturnalia* lasted only one day, but it was later extended to as many as seven. It began with a sacrifice at the temple of Saturn. Young pigs were killed and eaten the next day at a dinner where masters waited on their slaves.

Medicine

The Romans gained most of their knowledge of medicine from the Greeks. Hippocrates, a Greek doctor who lived in the 5th century BC, described all the illnesses he encountered and recorded how he treated them. His writings formed the basis of Greek and then Roman medical teaching. During the republic medical schools opened in Rome, and the organized teaching of medicine began. Doctors had to learn many skills, for Roman medical methods often combined scientific treatments and religious rituals. Some doctors trained in army hospitals. They learned about anatomy and surgery from the wounds of soldiers. This is what a hospital tent might have looked like.

Complex operations, such as setting broken bones and amputating limbs, were performed.

Operations were very painful because there were no anaesthetics. Patients drank wine to dull the pain.

Most doctors began their careers as apprentices to other physicians. They learned by watching the more experienced doctors.

Surgical instruments

Archaeologists have found evidence of bronze and iron instruments that doctors used. Some of them are shown here.

Instrument case

Scalpels

Forceps

Scoops

Needles

Tongs

Hooks

Treatments and remedies

Roman doctors used many kinds of remedies. They knew that people's health was affected by what they ate, and often advised patients to alter their diets. They knew the benefits of exercise, fresh air and regular visits to the baths.

Doctors also used medicines made from plants, minerals and animal substances. The remains of medicines have been found. It is hard to tell what they were made of and what they were used for, but we know about some of them because many documents about medicine have survived. Discorides, an army doctor, wrote a catalogue of 600 plants and 1000 drugs which he had tested on patients.

Eye infections were treated with ointments made with lead, zinc or iron. The sticks were often stamped with the maker's name.

The sap of certain plants was used to cure skin problems and snake bites.

Pill-box

Medicinal herbs were added to wine. The mixture was drunk to cure coughs and chest complaints.

Ingredients were sometimes ground in a pestle and mortar then made into pills.

68

A visit to the doctor

The richest Romans had personal physicians to look after them. Other wealthy patients could afford to pay doctors to visit them at home, but ordinary people had to go to a hospital or surgery. In the 1st century AD a sort of state health service began. Under this scheme, each town had a number of doctors who were exempt from tax. They could accept fees, but were expected to treat the poor free of charge. Some doctors saw patients in ordinary shops open to the street. Others had quieter rooms, like the one shown here.

Cabinet with scrolls containing medical writings

Garden for growing herbs used to make medicine

Examination couch

Writers on medicine advised the doctor how to behave so as to make the patient feel at ease. Here the doctor is examining a young child.

Boxes containing medicines and ointments

Surgical instruments

Other doctors

Archaeological evidence like this tombstone suggests that there were some female doctors. They probably worked as midwives, assisting women in childbirth.

Some doctors travelled from town to town, treating people at each place they came to. They probably carried medicines with them to sell to their patients.

Dental treatment was also available. Technicians riveted extracted teeth to gold bridges to form false teeth. This technique was probably invented by the Etruscans†.

Religion and medicine

The Romans linked religion and medicine because they believed that their deities had powers to heal people. To obtain cures, many Romans performed complex religious rituals, while others relied on superstition and spells. Some doctors used these treatments because they too held these beliefs.

Throughout the Roman world there were temples to Aesculapius, the god of medicine. They contained statues of the god, like the one above. People slept in shrines, believing that their dreams would tell them how to cure their illnesses.

If they were cured, people gave offerings to the gods. Some were stone models of the part of the body that had been healed. Others showed the deities themselves. This one shows Aesculapius and his daughter Hygieia, the goddess of healing.

There was a temple to Aesculapius on an island in the River Tiber. Slaves who were too old or ill to work were often left there. Claudius† granted them freedom. Later the temple became one of the first public hospitals.

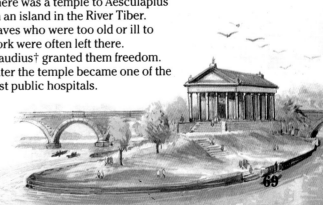

Architecture

In architecture, as in other areas, the Romans were influenced by the Greeks. They borrowed Greek styles, architects and craftsmen. However, the Romans were quick to adapt and develop Greek ideas. Their interest in architecture was mainly practical, and their great skills lay in the construction of huge buildings – amphitheatres†, baths, basilicas†, bridges and aqueducts†. The introduction of concrete enabled them to build stronger and bigger structures than before.

Temples

The Romans copied Greek temple architecture very closely. Greek temples were mostly built in open spaces and could be seen from all sides. Roman temples, however, were often constructed in town centres, surrounded by tall buildings, and only visible from the front. This picture shows the Maison Carrée, a Roman temple, built in the first century AD at Nîmes, France.

While the Greek pillars were detached from the rest of the temple, the Roman peristyle was joined to the inner room (*cella*). This made the *cella* more spacious.

Cella

The row of columns (called a peristyle) round the temple was adopted from the Greeks.

The temple was raised from the ground to make it look more impressive. A long flight of steps led to the porch.

Ionic (Greek)
Doric (Greek)
Composite
Corinthian (Greek)
Tuscan

The Romans used five types of column for temples and other public buildings. They were adapted from those used in Greek architecture.

Arches

Before the Romans, most buildings were constructed with walls and columns topped by beams of wood or stone (known as trabeated architecture). The largest known roof span built this way is 7.3m (25ft). The Romans used these methods for buildings like the Maison Carrée, but they also developed the arch and the vault, which had been used earlier by the Etruscans †. The arch enabled builders to span greater distances. The method of building an arch is shown here.

First an arch-shaped wooden support was placed between two columns of stone.

Then wedge-shaped stones (known as voussoirs) were placed around the support.

An arch was very heavy, so the pressure had to be taken by special supports known as buttresses. These were placed against the pillars.

The development of the arch enabled the Romans to build fine bridges and aqueducts, such as the Pont du Gard in France. In this case the hillside acted as a buttress.

For the Colosseum in Rome, shown here as it looks today, architects used arches to support the structure. The columns outside were only for decoration.

Vaults and domes

The Romans realized that a line of arches side by side could produce a tunnel vault to enclose large areas. But this allowed very little light to enter a building.

Later architects developed crossed vaulting by overlapping two tunnel vaults at right angles to each other. This was lighter in weight and easier to illuminate.

The groin vault was first used at the baths in Rome. Shown here is the *tepidarium* (warm room) at the Baths of Diocletian. This was transformed around AD1550 into the church of Santa Maria degli Angeli.

A further development of the arch was the dome, made by crossing a number of arches over each other to enclose a circular area.

The Pantheon

The best example of a Roman dome is the Pantheon in Rome. It was built in 25BC as a new form of temple, by Augustus's lieutenant Agrippa.

In this picture part of the dome has been cut away so that the details can be seen.

The Pantheon is also a good example of the Roman use of concrete. The Romans did not know about reinforcing concrete with metal, so they had to make it extremely thick to ensure its safety.

The problem of illumination was solved by leaving a hole 8.5m (almost 30ft) in diameter in the centre of the roof.

The weight of the dome is concentrated on a ring of voussoirs which form the hole.

The outside of the dome was covered with bricks and strengthened by frequent arches. Pumice stone was used in the concrete to make it lighter.

The dome is 43m (141.9ft) high and 43m (141.9ft) across. This huge structure is still the world's second largest dome.

The inside of the dome was lightened by recesses called coffers.

The exterior of the lower part of the building was covered in a coating of marble.

Building technology

We know that the Romans were highly skilled builders because so many of their constructions have survived into modern times. Their spectacular innovations in the fields of civil and mechanical engineering enabled them to construct vast, strong buildings and public works. Archaeological evidence tells us that the Romans chose the finest materials and devised many sophisticated construction methods to ensure that their buildings were safe and lasted many years. This is how a Roman building site might have looked; the scene shows some of the methods, materials and equipment they used.

Roman builders mostly used local supplies of wood and stone.

Interior walls in many houses were built from wooden frames which were filled with stones and cement. The finished wall was coated with a layer of plaster.

Wooden scaffolding was used to support builders and keep blocks of stone in place.

At first a soft volcanic rock called tufa was used, and later travertine, a fine stone from quarries at Tibur, 27km (over 16 miles) from Rome.

Later builders began using marble from Italy and Greece. Some buildings were decorated with mosaics† or coloured plaster.

This crane, driven by slaves in a treadmill, was linked to pulleys. It made the lifting and positioning of heavy objects easier.

Concrete

The use of concrete was developed in the 2nd century BC. The Romans discovered how to make an excellent mortar out of volcanic ash, and so were able to build very strong structures. The stages of building a wall are shown here.

First two low brick walls were built with a space between them.

The space was filled with a mixture of cement mortar and stones or rubble.

Once the concrete had dried, another wall could be built on top in the same way.

At the top the stones in the concrete were smaller and lighter.

Tiles and gutters were moulded from clay then baked to harden them. Every brick and tile had the name of the factory stamped on it.

Bricks were often laid in elaborate decorative patterns.

The Romans produced excellent bricks, often rather flat and small. Bricklayers were highly skilled.

Civil engineering

Roman roads, bridges, buildings and water systems were all carefully planned. The success of so many of these projects shows how well the Romans dealt with complex mathematical and technical problems. Below you can see some Roman advances in civil engineering.

The Romans needed a good water supply for public baths and lavatories. Water flowed into huge cisterns along aqueducts (pipes set into bridges or laid underground). It was then distributed through a complex system of lead or earthenware pipes.

Water power was used to turn chains of waterwheels. This is a reconstruction of a set of wheels near Arles in France which was used to drive flour mills.

Treadmills turned by slaves or oxen were used to raise water from underground shafts such as mines. The water collected in troughs at the top of each wheel. Each trough was emptied by the wheel above.

Bridge building

First a temporary bridge was built over a row of boats. Wooden stakes, chained together in circles, were driven into the river bed. The water was then pumped out of this space.

Blocks of stone were placed inside the stakes, forming the pillars to support the bridge. When the pillars were tall enough, wooden frames were fixed between them. Arches were then built on top of the frames.

Tools and equipment

Roman metalworkers and carpenters made excellent tools for builders. Here are some examples.

The *groma* was used to estimate straight lines to make sure that buildings and roads were straight.

Stonemason's square

Cutting tool

Tongs

Trowel

Axe

The legal system

The first document to describe the Roman legal system in detail, known as the Twelve Tables, was published in 450BC. It was a list of rules and statutes, and covered many aspects of the law. Although only a part of it has survived, we know it contained laws about money, property rights, family and inheritance, and public behaviour. There were also sections about court procedure, crimes and punishments. The legal system changed considerably over the years, but it continued to be based on the Twelve Tables throughout imperial times.

Courts and trials

Trials had to be set in motion by individuals, as the government itself did not prosecute people. Courts were managed in Rome by *praetores*†, and in the provinces† by governors. These men decided whether or not cases were worthy of trial, then chose the judge or tried the case themselves.

Anyone claiming that a crime had been committed had to summon the suspect to appear at court. People who did this gained great honour and prestige. In Rome, trials were held in basilicas† near the *forum*†. This is what a Roman court might have looked like.

Interesting or scandalous cases drew large audiences who often participated by shouting and jeering.

Trials themselves took place in the rooms off the main hall.

If the suspect refused to attend the court the accuser could use force to take him. This often led to fights before trials.

In serious cases the accused paid a lawyer (called an *advocatus*) to speak on his behalf. Good lawyers were highly respected.

In important cases a jury of up to 75 people was called. Jury members had to be citizens†.

Sometimes the accused put ashes in his hair and wore rags, or brought his weeping wife and children to court. This was to make the judge and jury feel sorry for him.

After everybody had spoken the jury decided by voting whether or not the accused had committed the crime. The judge announced the verdict and decided the punishment.

Crimes and punishments

Roman writings about law contain details of crimes and punishments. In imperial times the punishment depended on the status of the accused. Judges placed each defendant into one of two categories: *honestiores* and *humiliores*. The *humiliores* were usually poorer, and got worse punishments.

Many people were tried for crimes like not paying debts, not fulfilling contracts, or fraud. As punishment they had to pay fines or compensation.

Criminals were not imprisoned. Instead they were exiled to distant parts of the empire for a period. Others lost their citizenship and had their property confiscated.

Laws and lawyers

Roman law changed constantly throughout Rome's history. The legal system outlined in the Twelve Tables grew into a vast code of laws and their interpretations, from which a ruling could be found to suit most circumstances. This diagram shows how the law was put into practice.

Republican law

During the republic laws were made by the Senate† and the Assemblies†.

These laws were often imprecise, so judges had to decide how to apply them in court. This was part of a judge's skill.

When a judge took office, he issued a document called an *edictum*. It listed his interpretation of each law, and was based on that of his predecessor.

Verdicts and judgements were written down and explained, so legal books not only listed the laws but also advised on how to interpret them.

Governors took local customs into account when writing the *edictum*, so laws differed in each province.

Imperial law

During the Empire the system changed. Most new laws were devised by the emperor.

Other laws, though issued by the Senate, still had to be approved by the emperor.

Judges still issued edicts interpreting the law, but their powers were reduced.

Later, Hadrian† collected all the regional edicts and standardized them. A lawyer named Julianus Salvius was given the task of listing all the laws.

Augustus chose some eminent lawyers to give their opinions on legal matters. Judges had to follow these opinions when they conducted trials, and were not allowed to change or interpret individual laws.

Hadrian's reforms meant that all citizens† had to obey the same laws. In AD212 citizenship was granted to free men throughout the empire. This meant that the law applied to all Roman people.

Roman citizens throughout the empire could appeal to the legal authorities in Rome if they thought they had been wrongly tried or sentenced.

In republican times the death penalty was rare, but during the Empire crucifixion (death on a cross), flogging, beheading or drowning were more common.

Many *humiliores* who were sentenced to death had to appear in public games. They either fought as gladiators or were savaged by wild animals (see page 61).

Others were sent to be oarsmen on warships or to work in mines. The conditions were harsh and many prisoners died as a result of maltreatment and overwork.

The later Empire

After the rule of Marcus Aurelius (see page 25), political problems increased, caused by dishonest, brutal or incompetent emperors and rebellious soldiers. The Praetorian Guard† became very powerful, often choosing or deposing emperors without consulting the Senate†. This led to frequent changes of ruler, so the empire lacked the continuity and strong leadership it needed.

Commodus AD180-192; Pertinax AD192

Aurelius abandoned Nerva's method of choosing a successor (see page 25). Instead he appointed his son Commodus, who made peace with the barbarians†, but then ruled irresponsibly, ignoring the needs of the empire. He was murdered in

AD192. His successor, Pertinax, was killed after only three months by the Praetorian Guard, who auctioned the throne. The winner was Didius Julianus.

Didius Julianus AD192; Septimius Severus AD193-211

Three army groups on the frontiers became jealous of the Praetorian Guard's power. They chose their own emperor, Septimius Severus, who returned to Rome and deposed Julianus. Severus kept the barbarians out of the empire for 14 years, but he had to raise taxes to pay the army. For the first time even Romans in Italy were taxed.

Caracalla AD211-217

Caracalla, Severus's son, raised the army's wages again, and paid barbarians to stay away from the borders. He is remembered for the baths that he built in Rome. To increase the number of people he could tax, in AD212 he granted citizenship† to all free males in the empire. He was murdered by his Praetorian† Prefect, who seized power until he too was assassinated.

Bust of Caracalla

Elagabalus AD218-222

Elagabalus became emperor when he was 15. He was fanatically dedicated to worship of a Syrian sun-god. The Praetorian Guard killed him and chose his cousin Alexander as the new emperor.

Severus Alexander AD222-235

Alexander was only 13, so his mother Julia Mamaea ruled for him. She brought the army under control and gave management of the empire to a small group of senators. She also improved social conditions. Teachers and scholars were subsidised, as were landlords who repaired their property. Julia achieved relative peace, but after 12 years the eastern frontiers of the empire were invaded. The army rebelled against the government and murdered Alexander and Julia.

The Anarchy AD235-284

Chaos followed. The throne went to an army leader, Maximinus Thrax, a barbarian who could hardly speak Latin and had never been to Rome. After this the empire was torn apart by civil wars. Various army factions nominated more than 50 different rulers. Huge areas of the empire were ruined by famine, plague or invasion. Taxation was heavy and prices rose; many people left their homes to join bands of outlaws. Finally the wars ground to a halt, but the country was devastated.

Diocletian AD284-305

In AD284 Diocletian, a general in the Danube, was declared emperor by his troops. To establish order, he enlarged the army and made it responsible for the administration of the empire. Aware of the threat posed by ambitious soldiers, he increased the number of generals but gave each one fewer troops. He split the provinces† into smaller areas – 70 at first, later 116 – to make them easier to manage. More civil servants were appointed to handle the new administrative work.

Diocletian's most radical change was to divide the empire into two. Each half was governed by its own Augustus† and Caesar†. Diocletian was Augustus of the East, and set up his court at Nicomedia (see map). In AD286 another soldier, Maximian, was appointed Augustus of the West.

This statue represents the new system of leadership.

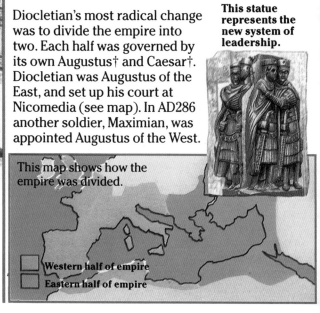

This map shows how the empire was divided.

☐ Western half of empire
☐ Eastern half of empire

To stop prices and wages rising, Diocletian issued lists of the maximum sums that people could charge for goods and labour. But this did not work. In addition, the cost of defending the empire made it necessary to increase taxes. To make taxation more efficient, a census† was taken every five years. At first people had to stay on their land while the census was counted; later they were forced to remain permanently where the census takers had first found them.

The empire ran much more efficiently, but people had less freedom. The law was enforced by the army, which as a result became very influential.

Soldiers were now less able to depose the emperor, but they had more power over ordinary people. The Senate lost most of its authority, and in effect simply became the city council of Rome.

Diocletian convinced the people it was the will of the gods that he was emperor, and declared himself a god. It was impossible for others to challenge him. In AD305 he resigned, persuading Maximian to do so at the same time. He retired to a huge palace which was built for him at Spalatum in Dalmatia (now Split in Yugoslavia).

Diocletian's palace

Diocletian expected the two Caesars to take over, but this arrangement did not last long before the army interfered. Once more soldiers tried to choose emperors to suit themselves. By AD311 there were four contenders for the throne.

Constantine AD312-337

One contender, Constantine, was leading the army in Britain. In AD312 he returned to Rome with his troops and defeated Maxentius, his main rival, at the Milvian Bridge. It is said that before the battle Constantine saw a cross in the sky and the words *'In hoc signo vinces'* ('You will conquer with this sign'). After his victory he granted tolerance to all religious groups, including Christians† (who under Diocletian had been badly persecuted).

Constantine adopted the Christian symbol shown on this tomb. It is made up of the first two letters of Christ's name in Greek: *chi* (χ) and *ro* (ρ).

Constantine began reuniting the empire. He defeated various rivals, and became sole emperor in AD323. He granted freedom of worship to Christians and gave people special privileges if they adopted the religion; in AD337 he formally became a Christian on his deathbed. Constantine demanded to be treated as the earthly representative of the Christian God, and began taking part in religious disputes and discussions. In this way he cleverly transferred the ideas of the state religion – that the emperor had divine status and religious authority – to Christianity.

Constantine wanted a new capital city to rival the splendour of Rome. In AD330 he moved his court to Byzantium, a former Greek colony at the entrance to the Black Sea, where he founded a new city called Constantinople (now Istanbul; see page 80). It remained an imperial capital for 1000 years.

Constantine was tolerant in religious matters, but he ruled in an authoritarian manner. The security of the empire depended on huge armies, and taxes had to be collected by thousands of civil servants. Workers were increasingly tied to their land and professions. But these measures still failed to halt the decline of the economy, and could not prevent the threat of the barbarians (see overleaf).

This head of Constantine, once part of a statue 10m (30ft) high, was probably an object of worship.

Key dates

AD180-192 Commodus

AD192 Pertinax, Didius Julianus

AD193-211 Septimius Severus

AD211-217 Caracalla

AD218-222 Elagabalus

AD222-235 Severus Alexander

AD235-238 Maximinus Thrax

AD238-284 Civil wars

AD284 Diocletian takes power.

AD286-305 Maximian rules western empire; Diocletian rules eastern empire.

AD293 Galerius and Constantius appointed Caesars; new system of government is formalised.

AD305-312 Struggles for power

AD312-337 Constantine (East and West united again from 324).

The Empire after Constantine

After Constantine's death the empire was divided among his three sons, but struggles for power soon arose. After the death of two of them the third son, Constantius II, reunited the empire, but himself died in AD361.

His successor, Julian (AD361-363), was known as the Apostate (someone who abandons one religion for another). Julian restored the old Roman gods and rebuilt their temples. Though Christianity † was not banned, people who worshipped the old state deities were favoured.

Julian was very hardworking and conscientious. He cut the number of palace workers and gave back independence to city councils throughout the empire. Julian's successor, Jovian (AD363-364), restored Christianity to its former supremacy.

Julian

Soon events outside the empire threatened its frontiers. The Huns, a tribe from eastern Asia, began moving west. They invaded the territory of other tribes, who in turn had to move further west to escape them. In AD367 the Visigoths†, Vandals† and Suebi began to set up their own kingdoms on Roman territory. This coincided with a series of short-lived emperors who were too weak to prevent the invasions.

Huns
Alamanni
Franks
Vandals
Ostrogoths
Visigoths
Western part of empire
Rome
Suebi
Eastern part of empire

This map* shows the movement of tribes c.AD367.

Barbarian soldiers

Theodosius fought against the break-up of the empire, and was the last emperor to rule both East and West. In theory Theodosius's sons were joint rulers of the whole empire, but they split it down the middle again and each ruled half. This scheme continued for another century; usually each emperor was succeeded by his eldest son. But these rulers were often interested only in personal power and wealth. Meanwhile the barbarians continued to advance, further contributing to the downfall of the western half of the empire.

Honorius AD395-423

During Honorius's rule the barbarians shattered the security of the empire. In AD402 Italy was invaded by a tribe of Goths led by a commander called Alaric. Scared by this, Honorius moved the imperial court to Ravenna on the east coast of Italy. Gradually Ravenna grew from a poor town into a properous city, and it remained an imperial centre for centuries.

Ivory plaque showing Honorius.

This is one of the oldest surviving buildings in Ravenna. It is known as the Baptistry of the Orthodox, and was built during the 5th century AD.

Theodosius AD379-395

During the frontier unrest, Theodosius took power (AD379). Unable to expel the barbarians from Germany, he made a treaty with them. This granted them safety if they provided soldiers and farm-workers for the Romans. Barbarian Germans, and later Huns themselves, became a regular part of the Roman army. Many Romans disliked this, but it was necessary as not enough Roman citizens were willing to become soldiers.

This silver relief shows Theodosius in his official robes.

While Honorius lived in splendour and safety until his death in AD423, the empire was being overrun by the barbarians. In AD409 the Vandals invaded Spain. In AD410 Rome was sacked by Alaric, who rapidly invaded the rest of Italy. That same year the Romans abandoned Britain and recalled the British legions† to defend the shrinking empire. Disease and famine weakened the population. It is also likely that people stopped wanting to fight the barbarians, because they no longer had any faith in a Roman government that kept taxing them and restricting their freedom.

The barbarians take over

The barbarians swept across Europe. Part of Gaul was occupied by the Burgundians†, and northern Europe by the Franks. In AD429 the Vandals moved from Spain to North Africa. In AD451 the Romans drove the army of Attila the Hun out of central France. But this was the last Roman victory.

The empire was continually under attack. In AD455 the Vandals sailed to Italy, invaded Rome and destroyed it. The city's administrative services collapsed. Chaos and famine followed. Rome's population fell from over 1 million to about 20,000. Romulus Augustulus, the last emperor of the West, was deposed in AD476 by Odoacer, a German captain who declared himself king of Italy and ruled from Ravenna. The western empire had ended.

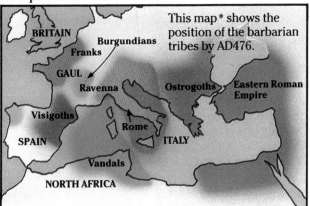

This map* shows the position of the barbarian tribes by AD476.

Many barbarians, such as the Vandals in Africa, were violent fighters who wanted to remove all trace of the Romans. Others, like the Burgundians, did not destroy the areas they conquered, and tried to preserve Roman buildings. But often they failed to do so because they did not have the skills to keep the buildings in good repair.

Each barbarian tribe ruled the area it conquered in its own way. Romans were badly persecuted in some areas. In others the invaders were tolerant. They could not keep strict control over large areas, so local Roman governments were able to preserve the Roman way of life for years. But in the West the idea of the empire, once so important to the Roman people, gradually faded away.

The rise of the Christian Church

In the 4th century AD the Christian Church became richer and more powerful. Educated men began to choose careers as religious officials rather than entering the army or politics. The Church began to influence the way the empire was governed. Bishops, not generals, organized resistance to the barbarians. They also converted many barbarians to Christianity. The developing Church produced many writers and philosophers. Even after the barbarian invasion the Church remained very influential.

This mosaic shows Ambrosius, a Roman bishop. He was highly respected for his teaching and writings.

As Christianity grew, Christians founded communities called monasteries all over the empire. In monasteries men called monks lived away from the rest of society and observed strict rules of behaviour. Some monasteries became famous places of learning, and monks saved and copied ancient books. In this way they preserved many works of Latin and Greek literature and history which otherwise might have been destroyed.

Key dates

AD337-361 Rules of Constantine II, Constans, and Constantius II.

AD361-395 Many emperors of East and West, including Julian ('the Apostate') and Jovian.

AD379-392 Theodosius rules as emperor of East.

AD392-395 Empire re-united under Theodosius.

AD395-423 Rule of Honorius.

AD402 Italy invaded by Alaric the Goth. Honorius moves the imperial court to Ravenna.

AD409 Vandals invade Spain.

AD410 Sack of Rome by Alaric.

AD455 Vandals invade Italy from Africa and destroy Rome.

AD476 Romulus Augustulus, last emperor of the West, is deposed by Odoacer.

*For a note about the projection of this map, see page 3.

The Byzantine empire

While the western half of the empire declined, the eastern half flourished. It preserved many of the traditions of the western Romans, including their administrative skills and military system, and the Christian† religion. The eastern empire after the fall of the West became known as the Byzantine empire, after the original Greek name for the area.

Constantinople's position (see map) made it an ideal link between Europe and Asia, and it became a great and powerful city at the centre of a huge empire. The eastern Church became almost as influential as the Roman Church, and eastern rulers dreamed constantly of reconquering the old Roman empire. Art and culture flourished in Byzantine times. Mosaics became very lavish, inlaid with polished glass and precious stones and metals.

Ravenna
Rome
Constantinople

This mosaic†, in the Church of San Vitale, Ravenna, shows Theodora, the wife of Justinian (see below). Ravenna became the base of the eastern Church in Italy.

Justinian AD527-565

Justinian was one of the greatest emperors of the eastern empire. His armies reconquered most of Rome's former territory in the West. But the cost of this was enormous, and many areas they recovered were delapidated after years of barbarian rule. The inhabitants did not care who ruled them. Except for the southern part of Italy, all the areas that Justinian regained were lost once more within a century.

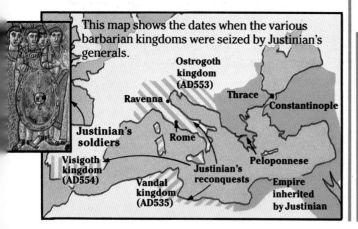

This map shows the dates when the various barbarian kingdoms were seized by Justinian's generals.

Ostrogoth kingdom (AD553)
Thrace
Ravenna
Constantinople
Justinian's soldiers
Rome
Visigoth kingdom (AD554)
Peloponnese
Justinian's reconquests
Vandal kingdom (AD535)
Empire inherited by Justinian

Justinian's most important achievement was his codification of the Roman legal system (see pages 74-75). This became the basis of the law throughout western Europe. He also launched a programme of building to enlarge and enhance Constantinople. This included the building of the Church of Santa Sophia (AD534-537). For centuries it was the largest church in the Christian world.

This reconstruction shows Santa Sophia as it might have looked in Byzantine times.

The later Byzantine empire

The eastern empire remained powerful for several centuries, but gradually links with Rome were broken. Latin was replaced by Greek as the official language, and the eastern Church and the Roman Catholic Church grew apart. The eastern Church was the forerunner of the modern Greek and Russian Orthodox churches.

The empire was soon challenged by Islam, the religion founded in Mecca, Arabia, by the prophet Mohammed (c.AD570-632). Within a century of Mohammed's death much of the old Roman empire had been conquered by the religion's followers, known as Muslims.

The Byzantine empire slowly shrank, until only Thrace and the Peloponnese were left (see map above). Constantinople itself was attacked by many different invaders and grew weaker and weaker, until it had very little political power. In AD1453 it fell to the Muslim armies of the Turkish Sultan Mehmet II. This event is seen by many historians as the point at which all remaining political links with imperial Rome were finally broken.

Key dates

AD491-518 Rule of Anastasius I, traditionally thought of as the first Byzantine emperor.

AD527-565 Rule of Justinian

AD528-534 Codification of the Roman law (known as the Justinian Code)

AD535 Justinian retakes the Vandal Kingdom in North Africa.

AD553 Justinian retakes the Ostrogoth Kingdom in Italy.

AD555 Justinian retakes the Visigoth Kingdom in Spain.

AD1453 Constantinople conquered by Sultan Mehmet II.

Glossary

Many Latin words in this book are listed and explained in the glossary below, which also contains some English words that may be unfamiliar. Other words related to the term appear in **bold** within the text of the entry. When a word in the text of an entry is followed by a dagger, that word has its own entry in this list. When the sign follows a name, see the 'Who's who' that begins on page 84.

Aedile. A government official. Four senators† were elected every year to become *aediles*. They were responsible for markets, streets and public buildings, and also organized public games.

Amphora. A large pot with two handles. *Amphorae* were used to transport and store oil and wine.

Amphitheatre. A circular or oval building in which gladiator fights and shows of wild beasts took place. The first amphitheatres were wooden; stone ones were later built all over the empire.

Aqueduct. A channel or pipe for carrying water. Rome and other cities of the empire had excellent supplies of water which was piped into urban centres from rivers and springs in the countryside. The pipes were either built underground or set into large bridges – also known as aqueducts – like the Pont du Gard in France.

Assembly. A meeting of Roman citizens† in Rome. **Assemblies** were held for various purposes, including the election of government officials, the passing or confirmation of laws, and the declaration of war or peace. The plebeians† also held their own **Popular Assembly**, which excluded patricians†, to elect their own representatives called tribunes†.

Atrium. The central area of a Roman house (*domus*†) on to which most of the other rooms opened.

Augustus. Imperial title. It was first taken by Octavian† when he became emperor† in 27BC. Later, under the system of succession devised by Nerva†, it was given to each new emperor when he took power. As the Augustus, the emperor chose a successor known as the Caesar†. The two men ruled together until the Augustus died. Then the Caesar took over, became the Augustus, and chose his own Caesar.

Barbarians. The name generally given to people who lived outside Roman territory. The Romans saw them as brutal and uncivilized because they did not conform to the Roman way of life. Invasions by various barbarian tribes was one cause of the collapse of the empire.

Basilica. A large public building, often near the *forum*† of a Roman town. It was used as law courts or offices, and sometimes also contained shops and markets.

Bulla. A good-luck charm. Each Roman child was given a *bulla* to keep evil spirits away.

Burgundians. People, originally from northern Europe, who around AD406 invaded the Roman empire and set up their own kingdom in the province† of Germania.

Caesar. Imperial title. Under the scheme of succession devised by Nerva†, each emperor decided who would take his place. The successor, until he himself became emperor, was given the title Caesar.

Cameo. A miniature carving in semi-precious stone.

Campus Martius. The Field of Mars, god of war. An open space near Rome where, in early republican† times, Roman armies assembled to go to war.

Carthage. A city on the coast of North Africa founded by the Phoenicians† about 814BC. The growth of **Carthaginian** power in Sicily caused the Punic† wars.

Cavalry. The part of an army that fights on horseback.

Censor. A government official. Two *censores* were chosen every five years. They served for 18 months; during this period they revised the membership of the Senate† and negotiated contracts for public works.

Census. A survey of the population. The Roman government gathered statistics and details about the inhabitants of the empire, mostly for taxation purposes.

Century. A unit of the Roman army. At first each century contained 100 men; later this was reduced to 80. Each century was led by an officer called a **centurion**.

Christianity. A religion founded in Palestine by the followers of the prophet Jesus of Nazareth (c.5BC-AD29), later known as Jesus Christ. His teachings spread rapidly through the Roman empire, though **Christians** were often badly persecuted until Christianity became the official state religion towards the end of the 4th century AD.

Citizen. A Roman man who had the rights to vote and to serve in the army. At first, to qualify for **citizenship** people had to be born in Rome to Roman parents. As the empire grew, however, the conditions were changed to include other people. Finally, in AD212, citizenship was granted to all men in the empire except slaves†.

Cohort. A unit of the Roman army. After the reforms of Marius†, a cohort became the main tactical unit. In each legion there were 10 cohorts; one contained 10 centuries, the others contained 6 centuries. It was led by an officer called a *tribunus militum*.

Consul. The most senior government official. Two consuls were elected each year; they managed the affairs of the Senate† and commanded the armies.

Contubernium. A unit of the Roman army. Each *contubernium* contained eight soldiers who ate together and shared a tent.

Denarius. A Roman coin. In early imperial times *denarii* were made from about 4 grams of silver.

Dictator. A government official. In times of crisis, such as during a war, the Senate† could appoint a dictator to rule for a maximum of six months. He was given complete control of all other officials and of the army, and took all important military and political decisions.

Domus. A private house, normally occupied by one family.

Emperor. The supreme ruler of all Roman territories. The first emperor was Augustus†, who took power in 27BC when the Roman republic† collapsed. The period after this date is known as the **Empire** (the capital letter is used in this book to denote 'the **imperial** period' rather than simply 'Roman territory').

Equites. A class of Roman citizen†. The *equites* were descendents of the first Roman cavalry† officers. In later republican† times the term denoted a powerful middle class of businessmen, traders and bankers.

Etruscans. People, perhaps originally from Asia Minor, who arrived in Italy about 800BC. The area they inhabited, in north-west and central Italy, is called Etruria. For parts of its very early history, Rome was ruled by Etruscan kings.

Forum. An open space at the centre of a Roman town. It was used for markets and trade, and was also the centre of social and political life.

Freed man. A slave† who had been released from slavery by his master.

Gauls. People who lived mainly to the north and west of Italy. There were many tribes of Gauls, who from around 500BC occupied much of what is now France, and areas as far north as the River Rhine and as far south as the Italian Alps. During the early republic† the Gauls attacked Rome frequently; by Caesar's time, however, most of them had been conquered. Their lands were seized by the Romans to form the various Gallic provinces†.

Goths. People who lived originally in Scandinavia. Around the beginning of the 1st century AD they began moving south, and by AD200 they lived north of the Black Sea. From here they attacked Roman territory in Asia Minor, but were defeated. Shortly after this they divided into two factions, known as the Visigoths† and the Ostrogoths†.

Hades. Originally, in Greek, the god of the dead. Later, for the Romans, the place where a person's spirit went after death. To reach Hades the spirit was rowed across a mythical river called the Styx by a boatman called Charon.

Huns. A tribe from eastern Asia who began moving west in the 4th century AD. They invaded the lands of the Ostrogoths†, Visigoths† and Vandals†, who had to move west into the Roman empire to escape them.

Hypocaust. A form of central heating. Buildings were constructed with spaces between the inner and outer walls and below floors. Fires were lit in special furnaces, and the heat flowed into these cavities.

Insula. A block of flats or apartments. Most occupants rented their living-quarters from a landlord. Each individual apartment was called a *cenaculum*.

Lararium. A shrine, kept either in the *atrium*† or garden of a *domus*†, which contained statues of the Roman household gods. The family said prayers at the *lararium* every day.

Latins. People, originally from central Europe, who entered Italy around 2000BC. They settled on the plain of **Latium** (an area of flat land on the north-west coast of the Italian peninsula which surrounds Rome).

Legatus. A government official. In republican† times *legati* worked in the provinces†, serving on the staff of the proconsul†. In imperial times *legati* commanded the legions or acted as military and political advisors or administrative assistants.

Legion. A unit of the Roman army. The size of the legion varied throughout Rome's history. It is thought that in the earliest times it was made up of about 3000 soldiers; by the 4th century BC this number had risen to about 4200. After the reforms of Marius† there were about 5000 soldiers in a legion.

The number of legions also varied. In late republican† times there were 60, but Augustus† cut this number to 28. After his rule there were always around 30 legions.

Ludi. The general name given to sporting events, public games and theatrical performances. Most *ludi* were held to mark religious festivals, funerals or battle victories.

Mosaic. A picture or abstract pattern made up of small pieces of stone, glass or glazed earthenware.

Nomads. People who do not live permanently in any one area but move from place to place.

Ostrogoths. A subdivision of the Goths† who built up a huge empire north of the Black Sea in the 3rd and 4th centuries AD. Around AD370 they were overrun by the Huns†, and so had to move west. From around AD455 they lived in the Balkans. They overran Italy in AD489, led by Theoderic, who deposed the barbarian ruler Odoacer and then declared himself king of Italy.

Paedagogus. A slave†, often Greek, employed by Roman parents to look after their children at school.

Papyrus. A reed used to make a form of writing material (itself often also called papyrus). It was cut into strips which were pressed, dried and polished to create a smooth writing surface.

Patricians. A class of Roman citizen†. Patricians were descended from the oldest families of noblemen. In early republican† times, only patrician men could become senators†. They also held all the most important political, religious and legal appointments.

Peristylium. A row of columns round a building or open space. The word is also used to mean an outdoor walkway or garden surrounded by a row of columns.

Phoenicians. People who lived in the eastern Mediterranean (now Lebanon) from around 1200BC. They were avid traders and sea-farers, and rapidly occupied many Mediterranean islands and parts of North Africa. Their most important colony was Carthage. The growth of Carthaginian power in Sicily caused the Punic† wars.

Plebeians. A class of Roman people. The plebeians were the poorest citizens† who were probably descended from Rome's first farmers and traders.

Praetor. A government official. At first the word was used for the two most important officials who replaced the kings at the beginning of the republic†. Later these men became known as consuls†; the word *praetor* instead came to mean the senior judges, administrative officers elected each year by the Assembly†, and governors in some of the provinces†.

Praetorian Guard. An army of around 9000 soldiers formed by Augustus†. It protected Italy and the emperor, as there were no legions† to do this. Because it was the only part of the army stationed in Rome, the Praetorian Guard became very powerful.

Proconsul. A government official. A proconsul was a consul† who, after his term of office, was sent by the Senate† to another job, usually as governor in one of the provinces†.

Province. From later republican† times (after the expansion of Roman territory), any area outside Rome (later outside Italy) that was controlled by the Romans. The inhabitants of these areas are known as **provincials**.

Punic wars. Three wars, fought at intervals from 264BC to 146BC, between the Romans and the Carthaginians. The word Punic is derived from the Latin word *Punicus*, meaning Phoenician†.

Quaestor. A government official. Twenty *quaestores* were chosen each year to be financial administrators.

Republic. A state or country without a king, queen or emperor which is governed by elected representatives of the people. Rome became a republic at the beginning of the 6th century BC when the last Etruscan† king was expelled. Though after this it was occasionally ruled by dictators†, it remained a republic until 27BC when Octavian† became emperor†.

Senate. The group of officials that governed Rome. In early republican† times the Senate consisted of around 100 patricians†; by 82BC there were 600 **senators**, selected from all classes of citizen†. The Senate took most political, military and legal decisions that related to Rome and Roman territory, but gradually the **senatorial** system broke down. After a period of dicatorships† and civil wars, Octavian† took power. During imperial times, the Senate's powers were gradually reduced as emperors took more and more power for themselves.

Slave. A person owned by another and used as a worker. In Rome most slaves were non-Romans, such as prisoners of war and their descendants. They were owned by citizens† or by the state, and were bought and sold like any other property. They had no rights or privileges, and were forced to work at any jobs their masters gave them.

Terracotta. A mixture of clay and sand, used to make tiles and small statues.

Toga. The official garment of a Roman citizen†. It was a roughly semi-circular piece of woollen cloth which the wearer draped around his body in an elaborate series of folds. The most popular colour was white; senators wore a *toga* with a purple border. Young boys also wore a *toga* with a purple hem, called the *toga praetexta*.

Tribune. An official elected by the plebeians† to represent them in the Senate† and protect their interests. In the first Popular Assembly† of 494BC two tribunes were elected; later this number was increased to ten. Tribunes could prevent any actions of the Senate or laws passed by magistrates if they believed that these threatened the rights of the plebeians.

Vandals. People who lived originally in Scandinavia. At the end of the 1st century BC they began moving south; by about AD200 they occupied an area south-west of the River Danube. In AD406, moving west to avoid the Huns†, they crossed the River Rhine into Gaul and devastated large areas of the country. In AD409 they entered Spain, where some of them settled; others moved on to North Africa. From here they sailed to Italy and in AD455 attacked and destroyed Rome.

Viaduct. A bridge built to carry a road across a river or a valley.

Villa. A large house in the country. Most villas were owned by rich city-dwellers who only visited the country from time to time. When the owner was absent the estate was run by a manager. Many villas were centres of farming or other industries.

Visigoths. A subdivision of the Goths† who settled in Dacia in the 3rd century AD. In AD376, escaping from the Huns†, they moved south across the River Danube and into Moesia. Led by Alaric, they advanced through Greece, continued to Italy and in AD419 attacked Rome. After this they moved to Gaul, and finally settled in Spain, where their kingdom survived until the 8th century AD.

Who was who in Ancient Rome

Below is a list of important Romans, with details of their lives and works. If a person's name appears in **bold** in the text of an entry, that person also has his or her own entry in this list.

Agrippina (AD15-59). Mother of **Nero**. She became involved in various political intrigues and was banished from Rome in AD39. Her uncle **Claudius**, however, allowed her to return and married her in AD49. She encouraged him to adopt Nero, her son by a previous marriage. It is said that she later poisoned Claudius so that Nero could become emperor. Later, when she opposed Nero's intention to marry Poppaea Sabina, Nero had her murdered.

Augustus. The title taken in 27BC by Octavian when he became the first Roman emperor†.

Octavian was the great-nephew and adopted son of Julius **Caesar**. After Caesar's death he formed an alliance with **Mark Antony** and Lepidus; the three men seized power and in 42BC defeated **Brutus** and his troops. When Lepidus retired, Octavian and Antony split Roman territory between them, but later disagreed. Octavian defeated Antony in the Battle of Actium in 31BC.

After so many years of civil war the Senate knew that Rome needed a strong ruler, so they gave Octavian command of the armies, sole control of foreign policy, and power to reform the Roman administration. He was given the title Augustus ('revered one') in recognition of his status as the head of the Roman government.

By working closely with the Senate and involving it in his decisions Augustus brought peace and prosperity to the Roman world after decades of unrest and civil war. In addition he reformed the army and made the provinces more secure. Building schemes were begun in Rome, and welfare was improved for the poor. According to **Suetonius**, Augustus was fair and honest; his rule was so successful that the idea of restoring a republican† government gradually died out.

Brutus (85-42BC). Politician, leader of the plot to murder **Caesar**. A famous soldier, and a firm believer in the ideals of the Roman republic†, he thought that Caesar was too powerful. Hoping to restore republican traditions, he and several others murdered Caesar in 44BC. After this he fled to Macedonia and later committed suicide.

Caesar, Julius Gaius (c.100-44BC). Politician, general and writer. He was born in Rome and was educated there and in Rhodes. He already had a reputation as a fine soldier when his political career began in 68BC. From 58BC to 49BC he led troops in Gaul and Illyricum, and extended Roman territory as far as the Atlantic coast and the English Channel. He recorded this period of his life, and details of his military campaigns, in seven books called *De Bello Gallico* (The Gallic Wars).

Disputes with Pompey and the Senate caused Caesar to return to Italy in 49BC, supported by his army. After defeating his enemies he became the most powerful man in Rome. He described these victories in three books called *De Bello Civili* (The Civil Wars). He was declared dictator† for life, but despite his popularity with the Roman people many senators believed he was too powerful. A group of these, led by **Brutus**, murdered him on 15 March 44BC.

Caligula. See **Gaius**.

Cato (234-149BC). Politician and writer. He fought in the second Punic† war, then held political positions in Sicily, Africa and Sardinia. In 184BC he was a censor†. Cato believed in the republican† values established when Rome was a small semi-rural settlement: restraint, dignity, and simple living. These are described in his book *De Agri Cultura*, which is the oldest existing work of Latin prose. He also wrote *Origines*, a history of the Roman people from the earliest times. His great grandson, also a politician, was one of Caesar's bitterest enemies.

Catullus (c.84-c.54BC). Poet. He settled in Rome as a young man. Details of his life, including travels to Asia and his final illness, are recorded in his poems. These include laments, witty parodies and elegant descriptions of incidents from Roman life. Catullus was one of the first Roman poets to adopt the forms and styles of Greek poetry.

Cicero (106-43BC). Politician, lawyer and writer. He was educated in Rome and Athens, and in 81BC his first speeches in the law courts earned him recognition as the greatest public speaker of his day. He became a famous lawyer, and was a consul† in 63BC. However he made political enemies by speaking out against people in the Senate and courts. After **Caesar**'s murder Cicero made many speeches in the Senate opposing **Mark Antony**. As a result, when Antony and **Octavian** took power, Cicero was murdered by their troops.

Many of Cicero's speeches were written down; they tell us a lot about life in late republican† times. His letters and philosophical writings also survive, and show that Cicero was responsible for introducing many Greek ideas to the Romans. His style of writing and speaking were imitated by scholars for centuries after his death.

Claudius (10BC-AD54). Emperor AD41-54. He was declared emperor by the army after the death of **Gaius**. Childhood illnesses had left him weak and crippled, and most of his relatives thought him stupid. But he was in fact very intelligent; contemporary accounts tell us he was a good public speaker, an excellent historian (he wrote several books of history, though none survives) and a wise and sympathetic ruler.

Constantine (c.AD274-337). Emperor AD312-337. He was leading the army in England when his father, the emperor Constantius, died. Constantine returned to Rome and defeated his rival for the throne, Maxentius, at the Milvian Bridge. Once in power he moved the imperial court from Rome to a new city on the Black Sea which he called Constantinople (now Istanbul). Constantine was the first Christian emperor; in AD313 he issued the Edict of Milan, granting freedom of worship to Christians.

Crassus (c.112-53BC). Soldier and politician. He defeated the uprising led by the slave Spartacus in 71BC, and was consul with **Pompey** the following year. In 60BC he joined an alliance with Pompey and **Caesar**; his extreme wealth enabled him to support Caesar's political ambitions.

Diocletian (AD245-313). Emperor AD284-305. He was declared emperor in AD284 by his troops. He made many radical reforms to coinage, taxation, the army and, most importantly, the way in which the empire was organized. After splitting Roman territory into two he ruled the East and appointed another emperor, Maximian, to rule the West. The administrative systems he devised, implemented by an expanded civil service, lasted for centuries.

Domitian (AD51-96). Emperor AD81-96. He took power after the death of his brother **Titus**, and quickly began to strengthen the frontiers of the empire to protect them from the barbarians. A patron of the arts, he also restored and improved many of Rome's buildings. But he was an arrogant ruler who did not respect the Senate. The end of his rule was marked by constant political quarrels. He solved these by ordering the murder of anyone who disagreed with him. He was eventually assassinated.

Gaius (AD12-41). Emperor AD37-41. He grew up in various military camps by the River Rhine, where his father was an officer. He was nicknamed Caligula because of the small soldier's boots (*caligae*) he wore as a child. **Suetonius** and others describe him as arrogant, cruel and extravagant. After ruling for four years in a wilful, inconsistent manner he was murdered by the Praetorian† Guard.

Hadrian (AD76-138). Emperor AD117-138. He succeeded his relative and adoptive father **Trajan**. A great soldier, he spent much of his rule with the armies in the provinces, and set up permanent barriers against the barbarians, including Hadrian's Wall in Britain. He was also a scholar and patron of the arts. He built a library in Athens and a villa for himself at Tibur near Rome. Around AD135 he set up an organization called the Athenaeum to sponsor writers and philosophers.

Horace (65-8BC). Poet. He was educated in Rome and Athens, then worked in Rome as a government clerk and began writing poetry. He became friendly with **Virgil**, and with Maecaenas, a patron of poets, who gave him a farm where he settled to write. **Augustus** asked Horace to be his secretary, but he refused. From their letters, however, it appears that the two men were friends. Horace's most famous works are the *Odes*, short poems on various subjects including the joys of the country, food and wine. His poetry became famous almost immediately and has remained widely read and studied.

Julian (AD332-363). Emperor AD360-363. On becoming emperor he began to restore worship of the ancient Roman deities, going against the official religion of the state which was by that time Christanity. He is known as 'the Apostate' – someone who abandons one religion for another. He greatly reduced his palace staff and improved the civil service, but was unpopular because of his religious views. He was killed fighting in Persia. Some of his letters and other writings survive, which give us details of political and religious life at that time.

Justinian (c.AD482-565). Emperor of the East, AD527-565. His most important political achievement was to recapture many of the territories in the West that had been overrun by barbarians. He also commissioned a huge codification of the Roman legal system, which formed the basis of his reforms of the political administration.

Juvenal (c.AD60-c.AD130). Poet. Almost nothing is known about his life. The first of his poems still in existence were probably published around AD110. His works are called *Satires*; they criticise what Juvenal saw as the evils and defects of life in Rome – poverty, immorality and injustice. The attacks, though bitter, are delivered with biting humour and wit. It is thought that his poems led to him being banished from Rome for a time.

Livia (58BC-AD29). Wife of **Augustus**, and, by an earlier marriage, mother of **Tiberius**. She was an aristocrat from one of the oldest Roman families, and had considerable influence on Augustus's rule. Roman historians tell us she was shrewd and wise; it is possible that she persuaded Augustus against his will to appoint Tiberius as his successor.

Livy (59BC-AD17). Historian. He spent much of his life in Rome writing *Ab Urbe Condita*, a huge history of the city and its people. It was published in instalments and brought him wealth and fame. It charts the development of Rome from the earliest times, and provides us with much detail of both historical incidents and everyday life.

Marcus Aurelius (AD121-180). Emperor AD161-180. Much of his rule was spent at the empire's frontiers, trying to keep the barbarians out. Aurelius's journals, known as *Meditations* and written mostly in army camps, show him to have been a peace-loving, philosophical man.

Marius (157-86BC). Soldier and politician. He fought successful campaigns in Spain, Africa and Gaul. During this period he was consul† six times (107BC, 104-100BC) and used his power to reform the army and make it more efficient. After this he was hardly involved in political life until 88BC, when tensions arose between him and **Sulla**. The struggle for power between the two men was one of the causes of the civil war that brought about the collapse of the republic†. Marius seized control in 87BC and the following year was appointed consul for the seventh time just before his death.

Mark Antony (82-30BC). Soldier and politician. He was a consul† with **Caesar** in 44BC. After Caesar's death he formed an alliance with **Octavian**; they split Roman territory and Antony ruled Egypt with his lover Cleopatra, the Egyptian queen. Later the two men disagreed and war broke out between them. Antony and Cleopatra committed suicide after their defeat by Octavian at the Battle of Actium.

Martial (c.AD40-AD104). Poet. He was born in Spain, and lived in Rome for many years. His poems, known as *Epigrams*, provide details of everyday life and describe some of Rome's more colourful characters. While much of his work is bitterly satirical, attacking various individuals for their faults, his writings also include poems to his friends and touching laments.

Nero (AD37-68). Emperor AD54-68. At first Nero's rule was effective and stable, but he freed himself from the influence of his advisors (including **Seneca**) and became arrogant and obsessed with power. Anyone who opposed him was murdered (including his mother **Agrippina**). According to **Suetonius** he sponsored public shows and games in which he himself appeared, and had to increase taxes to pay for them. It is thought that he caused the fire that destroyed much of Rome in AD64, and then began organized persecution of Christians, blaming them for the blaze. Eventually he left Rome and was forced to commit suicide.

Nerva (c.AD30-98). Emperor, AD96-98. He was appointed emperor by the Senate after **Domitian** was assassinated. A respected lawyer, he restored faith in imperial rule by treating the Senate and others with consideration. The army, at first uneasy about his appointment, was won over when he chose a famous soldier, **Trajan**, to succeed him. Nerva is best remembered for devising this system of succession (after him each emperor chose and trained his own replacement), and for increasing aid to the poor.

Octavian. See **Augustus**.

Ovid (43BC-AD18). Poet. He was educated in Rome and studied to become a lawyer, but gave this up to write poetry. His work became very popular in Rome, and he was friendly with **Horace** and others. In AD8, however, he was banished to the shore of the Black Sea by Augustus; the reason for this is not entirely clear, but he never returned to Rome. His most famous work is *Metamorphoses*, fifteen books of poems on a variety of subjects, chiefly legends or myths, all involving changes of shape and character. Ovid's poetry is notable for its pictorial detail; his writing later influenced many artists, including Rubens and Picasso.

Petronius Arbiter (lived 1st century AD). Author. Little is known about his life, but several of his works survive. The most famous of these is the *Satyricon*, a rambling narrative about the experience of three characters as they travel through southern Italy. The work is most important as a report on the social customs of the day, and as a description of the lives of people of various classes; it also contains historical poems and snatches of political commentary.

Plautus (c.254-184BC). Playwright. He is said to have written more than 130 plays, though only 21 survive. These are all based on Greek comedies, but introduce features of Roman life, often affectionately parodied, probably to make them more interesting to Roman audiences. The works of Plautus have inspired many later playwrights, particularly Shakespeare and Molière.

Pliny (c.AD61-c.113). Writer and lawyer. During **Trajan**'s rule he served as a consul†. He published nine volumes of his correspondence with the emperor, his friend **Tacitus** and others. Written in a clear, elegant style, they are an excellent source of information about the Roman world at that time.

Plutarch (AD46-126). Writer. He was born in Greece, but later lived in Rome. Many of his writings survive. They cover several different subjects, including science, literature and philosophy. His most famous work, known in English as *Plutarch's Lives*, is a series of biographies of Greek and Roman soldiers and statesmen. They are grouped in pairs, one Greek, one Roman, and their lives and careers are carefully compared.

Pompey (106-48BC). Soldier and politician. He fought with **Sulla** against **Marius**, and later suppressed the slave rebellion led by Spartacus. Asia Minor was added to Roman territory as a result of his campaigns there. He joined an alliance with **Caesar** and **Crassus** in 60BC, and remained in Rome while Caesar was fighting in Gaul. Owing to political tensions the alliance broke down, and in 49BC Caesar returned to Rome and seized power. Pompey was defeated and died in Egypt.

Seneca (c.5BC-AD65). Writer, philosopher and lawyer. He was born in Spain, but spent most of his life in Rome. In AD41 he was banished by **Claudius**, but was recalled by Agrippina eight years later to be **Nero**'s tutor. For a time Nero governed well, probably because of Seneca's influence, but the administration deteriorated and in AD62 Seneca asked to retire. Three years later he was accused of being involved in a conspiracy against Nero, and was forced to commit suicide. Seneca's most famous works are the *Apocolocyntosis*, a satire on the deification of Claudius, and his *Moral Letters*, which outline his philosophical beliefs.

Sibyl. A name used by the Greeks and Romans for several prophetesses active all over the Ancient World. One of them offered nine books of her prophecies to Rome's early king Tarquinius Priscus. When he refused to buy them, she burned three books and offered him the remaining six. Priscus refused again; the Sibyl burned another three books and offered the last three at the original price for nine. Priscus bought the books, which were kept in Rome by special priests; they were thought to be so sacred that they could only be consulted in extreme emergencies.

Suetonius (c.AD69-AD140). Historian. After a period as a lawyer he became a government assistant to **Trajan**, Hadrian and others. His most famous work is *Lives of the Twelve Caesars*, which has survived in complete form. It discusses the careers of each Roman ruler from **Caesar** to **Domitian**. As well as studying the political careers of the emperors, it also passes on a wealth of detail about their personalities, appearances, families and habits. In addition Suetonius also recorded the gossip, scandal and rumours surrounding the lives of his subjects.

Sulla (138-78BC). General and politician. His first military successes were as a lieutenant to **Marius**, who later became his fiercest rival. Between 88 and 86BC the two men were involved in constant struggles for power; after Marius's death in 86BC Sulla and his troops seized control of Rome and he declared himself dictator†. A man of highly conservative views, he tried to return power to the Senate and the patricians†.

Tacitus (c.AD55-c.AD116). Historian. He served as a military officer and held several government posts, including consul†. According to contemporary sources he was an excellent public speaker. His most famous works are the *Annals* (about the period from **Tiberius**'s rule to the death of **Nero**) and the *Histories* (about the lives of the emperors from Galba to **Domitian**).

Terence (c.195-159BC). Playwright. He was a slave†, freed by his master. His six plays – including *Phormio* and *Adelphoe* – were adapted from Greek comedy. Contemporary sources tell us that many audiences found Terence's plays dull, possibly because they are less exuberant than those of **Plautus**. But his work was performed in imperial times, and was known in the middle ages. Many later writers, including Sheridan and Molière, were inspired by his plays.

Tiberius (42BC-AD37). Emperor AD14-37. He had already retired to Rhodes when he was recalled to Rome in AD2. Twelve years later he became emperor. He appears to have been an excellent administrator, but many of his reforms were very unpopular. Terrified of being assassinated, he withdrew to the island of Capri and ruled through his deputy, Sejanus. Eventually Sejanus tried to seize power for himself, and Tiberius had him executed. After this he became suspicious and tyrannical. Anyone who he thought opposed him was forced to commit suicide.

Titus (AD39-81). Emperor AD79-81. He was the elder son of Vespasian, and had a distinguished military career. His capture of Jerusalem in AD70 is depicted on a triumphal arch in Rome. According to **Suetonius** he was extremely popular, generous and merciful. He gave financial aid to people who had suffered in the volcanic eruptions at Herculaneum and Pompeii (AD79) and in a huge fire in Rome (AD80). The Colosseum in Rome and other public buildings were completed during his term of office.

Trajan (?AD53-AD117). Emperor AD98-117. He was born in Spain and was an outstanding soldier and general; his military successes are commemorated on a huge sculpted pillar in Rome known as Trajan's Column. During his rule the empire grew to its largest with the conquest of Dacia and Parthia. Among his public works at Rome were baths, markets, a basilica and a new forum.

Vespasian (AD9-AD79). Emperor AD70-79. He came to power after the murder of **Nero** and the short rules of Galba, Otho and Vitellius. Rome was in civil and financial turmoil, but he quickly restored order. His improvements of the administration and the army achieved political stability, and he began an extensive programme of public building. This included the Colosseum, temples and restorations to the forum and elsewhere.

Virgil (70-19BC). Poet. He was educated at Cremona, Milan, and Rome. His first published work, the *Eclogues*, is a series of poems about life in the country. In 42BC his land was confiscated to provide farms for retired soldiers, and he lived for a time near Rome, and later near Naples and elsewhere. He completed his next great poems, the *Georgics*, in 30BC. During the last 10 years of his live he worked on the *Aeneid*, a poem in twelve books about the origin and growth of the Roman empire.

Vitruvius (c.70BC-early 1st century AD). Architect and engineer. He is most famous as the author of *De Architectura*, a series of ten books about architecture and building. They include information about civil engineering, construction, town-planning and materials, as well as sections about the techniques and styles of decoration. *De Architectura* brought together much information about Ancient Greek architecture, and is the only work of its kind to have survived ancient times.

Date chart

This chart lists the most important dates in Roman history. It also includes some events that took place elsewhere in the world during the same period; these are shown on indented lines.

Dates BC

from c.2000BC   Immigrants enter Italy from the North.

c.900BC   First settlements on Palatine and Esquiline hills.

> **c.900BC**   State of Sparta founded in Greece.

c.800BC   Etruscans arrive in Italy by sea.

> **776BC**   First Olympic Games held in Greece.

753BC   Date traditionally given for the founding of Rome. The city is ruled by a series of kings, some of whom are Etruscan.

c.750BC   Greek migrants settle on the southern coasts of Sicily and Italy.

> **c.650BC**   First coinage appears in Lydia (Asia Minor).

> **c.550BC**   Cyrus the Great founds Persian Empire.

510 or 509BC   Last king expelled from Rome; republic formed.

> **c.505BC**   Democracy established in Athens by Cleisthenes.

496BC   Romans defeated by an alliance of Latin cities at the Battle of Lake Regillus.

494BC   Plebeians go on strike for the first time.

> **494BC**   Ionian revolt crushed by Persians.

493BC   First two tribunes appointed.

> **490BC**   Battle of Marathon: Persians defeated by Greeks.

> **486BC**   Death of Siddhartha Gautama, founder of Buddhism.

450BC   Publication of the list of Roman laws known as the Twelve Tables.

> **450BC**   Celtic La Tène culture appears in Europe.

449BC   Number of tribunes increased to ten.

> **431-404BC**   Peloponnesian War, fought between Athens and Sparta.

by 400BC   Rome has become the dominant partner in the Latin alliance.

367BC   Law is passed declaring that one consul must be a plebeian.

366BC   First plebeian consul is elected.

338BC   Romans defeat the other members of the Latin alliance; the alliance is terminated.

> **334BC**   Alexander the Great invades Asia Minor. He conquers Egypt in 332, Persia in 330 and by 329 has reached India.

326BC   War breaks out between the Romans and the Samnites.

> **323BC**   Death of Alexander the Great in Babylon.

312BC   The Appian Way is begun.

287BC   Lex Hortensia passed, stating that all resolutions of the Popular Assembly should become law.

286BC   Final defeat of the Samnites.

280-272BC   Pyrrhic wars.

by 264BC   Rome dominates the whole of Italy

264-241BC   First Punic war.

241BC   Sicily becomes the first Roman province.

238BC   Romans seize Sardinia.

220BC   Via Flamina built.

218-202BC   Second Punic war.

> **214BC**   Great Wall built in China.

204BC   Rome invades Africa.

202BC   Rome seizes Carthaginian territory in Spain.

179BC   First stone bridge built over the River Tiber.

> **171-138BC**   Reign of Mithriades I of Parthia, who extends Parthian empire to Persia and Mesopotamia.

> **from c.170BC**   Greeks establish small settlements in parts of the Punjab, India.

149-146BC   Third Punic war ends with the destruction of Carthage.

133BC   Rome acquires the province of Asia. Tiberius Gracchus becomes tribune.

123BC   Gaius Gracchus becomes tribune.

121BC   Province of Gallia Narbonensis acquired.

107BC   Marius becomes consul, and begins reforms of the army.

88BC   Sulla marches on Rome and drives Marius into exile.

87BC   Marius recaptures Rome, but dies the following year.

82-80BC   Sulla is dictator.

73-71BC   Rebellion of discontented slaves, led by Spartacus.

70BC   Crassus and Pompey are consuls.

63BC   Pompey acquires provinces of Bythnia, Pontus, Cyrene, Syria and Crete.

59BC   Caesar is consul.

58-49BC   Caesar's campaigns in Gaul.

55-54BC   Caesar's invasions of Britain.

53BC   Death of Crassus.

49BC   Caesar returns to Rome and seizes power. Civil war breaks out between him and the Senate's forces (led by Pompey).

48BC   Pompey is killed in battle.

45BC   Caesar finally defeats the Senate's forces and becomes sole leader of the Roman world.

44BC   Caesar is assassinated by Brutus and Cassius.

42BC   Deaths of Brutus and Cassius.

c.33BC   Growing tension between Octavian and Mark Antony leads to civil war.

31BC   Octavian defeats Antony and Cleopatra at the Battle of Actium.

27BC   Octavian becomes first Roman emperor, and is given the title Augustus.

> **c.5BC**   Birth of Jesus Christ in Bethlehem, Judaea.

Dates AD

AD14   Death of Augustus. Tiberius becomes Emperor.

AD14-37   Rule of Tiberius.

AD17   Death of the historian Livy.

AD37-41   Rule of Caligula.

AD41-54   Rule of Claudius.

AD43   Conquest of Britain.

AD54-68   Rule of Nero.

AD64   Rome burns down; Nero begins persecution of Christians, blaming them for the fire.

AD68-9   After Nero's death, struggles for power lead to civil wars.

AD69   Reigns of Galba, Otho, Vitellius, before Vespasian takes power.

AD69-79   Rule of Vespasian.

AD79   The Colosseum in Rome, one of the empire's largest amphitheatres, is opened.

AD79-81   Rule of Titus.

AD79   The volcano Vesuvius erupts, destroying the towns of Herculaneum and Pompeii on the west coast of Italy.

AD81-96   Rule of Domitian.

AD96-98   Rule of Nerva.

AD98-117   Rule of Trajan.

AD112   Trajan's forum in Rome is completed.

AD117   The empire reaches its largest extent after the conquests of Dacia and Parthia.

AD117-138   Rule of Hadrian.

AD122   Building of Hadrian's Wall and other frontiers begins.

AD138-161   Rule of Antoninus Pius.

AD161-180   Rule of Marcus Aurelius.

AD180-192   Rule of Commodus.

AD193-211   Rule of Septimius Severus.

AD211-217   Rule of Caracalla.

AD212   Roman citizenship granted to all free people throughout the empire.

AD217-218   Rule of Macrinus.

AD218-222   Rule of Elagabalus.

AD222-235   Rule of Severus Alexander.

AD235-284   Short reigns of many emperors. Barbarians threaten the empire's borders. Plague and famine sweep through Europe.

AD260-275   Gaul declares independence from Rome.

AD270   Romans begin to abandon parts of the empire, withdrawing from Dacia.

AD271-5   The Aurelian Wall is built around Rome.

AD284   Diocletian takes power and splits empire into two parts, East and West.

AD284-305   Rule of Diocletian (East).

AD286-305   Rule of Maximinian (West).

AD286   Britain declares itself independent from Rome (until AD296).

AD301   Edict of maximum prices issued to regulate inflation.

AD305-312   Rule of Constantius I, followed by struggles for power which end when Constantine defeats Maxentius at the Battle of the Milvian Bridge.

AD312-337   Rule of Constantine. Empire is reunited from AD324.

AD313   Constantine issues Edict of Milan, tolerating Christian worship.

AD330   Constantine moves his court to Byzantium, where he founds the city of Constantinople.

AD337   Constantine baptised into Christian faith.

AD337-361   Rule of Constantine's sons.

AD361-363   Rule of Julian the Apostate; old state religion restored.

AD363-364   Rule of Jovian. Christianity restored.

AD364-379   Rules of Valentinian I, Valens, Gratian, Valentian II.

AD367   Barbarian tribes, moving west to escape the Huns, begin to set up their own kingdoms on Roman territory.

AD379-392   Theodosius rules as emperor of the East.

AD392-395   Empire re-united under Theodosius.

AD394   Christianity becomes official state religion.

AD395-423   Rule of Honorius.

AD402   The Goths invade Italy. Honorius moves the imperial court from Rome to Ravenna.

AD404   First Latin version of the Bible (known as the Vulgate) is completed.

AD406   The River Rhine freezes, allowing the Goths to cross it and enter Roman territory.

AD409   Vandals invade Spain.

AD410   Sack of Rome by Alaric the Goth. Rome abandons territories in Britain and Gaul.

AD449   Angles, Saxons and Jutes invade Britain.

AD455   Vandals invade Italy from Africa and destroy Rome.

AD475   Visigoths declare an independent kingdom in Spain.

AD476   Romulus Augustulus, last emperor of the West, is deposed by Odoacer, a barbarian captain who delcares himself king of Italy.

AD486   Clovis founds Frankish kingdom.

AD491-518   Rule of Anastasius I, traditionally thought of as the first Byzantine emperor.

AD527-565   Rule of Justinian.

AD535-555   Justinian's troops recapture much of the former Roman empire from the barbarians, but these territories are later lost again.

AD1453   Constantinople is conquered by Sultan Mehmet II.

The legacy of Rome

The Roman empire in western Europe came to a close in AD476 when the last emperor in Italy, Romulus Augustulus, was deposed. But the Roman way of life was so widespread and firmly established that it did not simply disappear when the barbarians took over. Some elements of Roman civilization remained as strong as ever after the fall of the empire, and had a huge impact on the cultures that followed them. Other aspects of Roman life – chiefly ideas and literature – all but disappeared in the middle ages. But they were maintained for centuries in monasteries and other centres of learning until they were rediscovered by writers, artists and scholars.

The Romans also transmitted to us skills and ideas learned or borrowed from other ancient cultures. Without the Romans, much information about more remote civilizations would be lost. Greek sculptures and many Greek writings exist almost solely in the form of Roman copies. Technical innovations of other ancient peoples only survive because they were adopted by the Romans. Below are examples of the ways in which the influence of the Roman world continues to be felt today.

Towns and cities

Much of western Europe had no urban civilization before the Romans, and they profoundly influenced its geography. They nearly always chose excellent positions for the towns they created, assessing physical and political factors before beginning to build. Many modern cities occupy the sites they do only because the Romans built there first, or developed tiny hamlets into large, prosperous towns. These include London, Paris, Lyons, Bordeaux, Cologne, Toledo, Milan and, of course, Rome itself.

Some European town centres are still laid out as the Romans planned them, with a large open space at the centre corresponding to the *forum* and roads that intersect at right angles. Bridges, markets and other public landmarks often occupy the sites where the Romans first placed them. In addition, other cities built or rebuilt long after Roman times were created by town planners in imitation of the grid pattern of the Greeks and Romans; these include New York and Lisbon.

Travel and communications

The Romans established trade and military routes all over Europe and into North Africa and Asia. Many can still be seen in ruins; far more, though no longer in existence, form the basis of modern main roads and railways, their directions being followed by modern planners. In addition, the wheel-gauge of Roman wagons became fixed at about 143 cm once ruts were worn in their roads. This is now the gauge of many railways, as early steam trains were tested on tracks in mines developed by the Romans.

Architecture

Very few barbarian tribes were able to maintain Roman buildings, and some actually destroyed them. Cities fell into disrepair and were plundered for stone and marble. But many Roman buildings lasted because they were so well made. The Romans' innovations and developments in architecture and building technology – the arch, the dome and the use of concrete – enabled them to create huge structures that still survive. Some are still in use, like the Pantheon in Rome and theatres and amphitheatres all over southern Europe.

In centres where building continued after Roman times, such as parts of the Eastern empire and certain cities in Italy, architects at first imitated the great buildings of Rome. Later in the Byzantine world architectural styles gradually changed, but many buildings were still based on the large domes and basilicas of late Roman times. In addition, many Roman basilicas were turned into churches during this period.

During the Renaissance (see opposite) Italian architects like Palladio (1518-80) discovered the books of the Roman architect Vitruvius. These codified the rules and styles of the classical architecture of the Greeks and Romans. Renaissance architects followed these guidelines; some copied Roman buildings in their entirety, others incorporated the rules into new designs. In addition, at this time many original Roman buildings were restored. The Baths of Diocletian in Rome, for example, were turned into the church of Santa Maria Degli Angeli by the Renaissance artist Michaelangelo.

Though new styles of architecture later developed, many architects continued to use Greek and Roman principles of proportion and design. In the 19th century many civic monuments were built with columns, domes and arched halls in an attempt to capture the imposing grandeur of ancient Rome. The National Gallery in London and the Louvre in Paris are good examples, but the European imperial powers also constructed buildings like this in many parts of the world, including India, Africa and Asia. Some large state buildings in the USA, including the Capitol in Washington, DC, also follow this style.

Painting and sculpture

In Renaissance times artists became fascinated with the classical statues (mostly Greek but preserved in Roman copies) that were being rediscovered. Michaelangelo and others adopted their realistic style and their proportions and moods, often altering them subtly to suit their own purposes. Myths and legends from the classical world were often used as the basis for paintings by such artists as Botticelli. At that stage, however, very few Roman wall-paintings had been found; when, in the 18th century, excavations began at Pompeii, classically inspired painting and sculpture received a fresh impetus. The classical legacy remains a source of inspiration for many modern artists.

Language

When the Romans conquered a new area, its inhabitants had to learn the language of their conquerors, because the new administration was conducted in Latin. This was not the language of literature or public speaking, but the everyday speech of peasants and soldiers. It survived after the fall of the empire, spoken all over the Roman world in various provincial forms. These dialects, when later fused with the languages of the barbarian invaders, grew into the modern European languages. Many of them – particularly Portuguese, Italian, French, Spanish and Romanian – are very closely linked to Latin. Others, like English, are more distantly related, but still contain thousands of Latin words.

A more formal, official Latin was preserved by the Christian Church. All church ceremonies were conducted in Latin, and it was the language spoken in monasteries. As these places were the main centres of learning during the middle ages, Latin became the language of scholars. By the 16th century Latin was used all over Europe by scholars, diplomats and scientists. This tradition has survived into modern times; a qualification in Latin is still an entrance requirement for some universities and colleges, whatever subject the student intends to study.

Law

The Roman legal system survived the collapse of the empire for many reasons. It was widely established, well integrated into Roman society on a local level, and meticulously codified and documented. The Romans' ideas of justice and rights, as outlined in the Justinian Code, (AD528-534), remain relevant today. Some modern legal systems, such as that in France, are based in a large part on the Justinian Code; others, though now very different from it, still display their origins in the Roman system. In the USA, the state law of Louisiana still follows Roman law very closely.

Government

The concept of an empire – a territory unified by one set of laws and governed by a central body – was not a Roman invention. The Macedonian ruler Alexander the Great conquered large parts of the eastern Mediterranean and Asia, hoping to unite them under a single political administration, but died before he could carry this out. The Romans not only acquired a vast empire but also succeeded in governing it smoothly and effectively. The Romans brought many benefits to the areas they conquered: improved buildings; trade; a legal system; and the vast economic resources of the empire.

The imperialist system was later copied by many rulers, with varying degrees of success. In AD800 the Frankish king Charlemagne was crowned 'Emperor of the Romans', in imitation of earlier Roman rulers. Later Frankish and German leaders continued this tradition, and named their territories the Holy Roman Empire. This institution remained in existence in Germany until 1806. Though Roman in name only, it demonstrates the potency of the Roman empire as a historical model.

In the 18th century the revolutionary movements in France and America were inspired by the ideals of the Roman republic to overthrow monarchic rule. The USA is still governed by a body called the Senate. By the 19th century some western European countries had empires all over the world, to which they, like the Romans, tried to export their culture and governmental systems. In modern times the European Community can be seen as an extension of the Roman ideal; it aims to bring the various member states together with a common monetary and taxation system, a central government, and an international court of justice.

Elements of Roman local government survive today in the Roman Catholic Church. Its managerial units, known as dioceses, were invented by Diocletian for civic purposes and only later adopted by the church. The idea of a religious empire with its own leader – the Pope – and its own laws is itself derived from the Roman imperial administration.

Literature and ideas

The great works of Latin literature, and histories of the Romans written by Romans themselves, were preserved in the middle ages by monks, who collected ancient books and copied the original manuscripts. From the 13th century there was a steady drift to the West of monks from the fast crumbling Byzantine world. The books they brought with them provoked new interest in Greece and Rome; this in turn brought about gradual cultural changes (first in Italy, later throughout Europe) known collectively as the Renaissance.

The Renaissance influenced all aspects of European life. Greek and Roman writings taught Renaissance thinkers to stress human possibilities rather than dwell, as most medieval theorists did, on human failings. Learning began to develop independently of the Church; schools and universities were founded by bankers, statesmen and others in non-religious walks of life. Scientific and medical experiments flourished. The political, religious and technological changes of this period mark the end of the medieval age.

Renaissance poets like Petrarch and Boccaccio imitated Latin verse forms (particularly those of Virgil); the Dutch scholar Erasmus perfected his Latin prose style by detailed study of Cicero. In this way writers incorporated Latin styles and ideas into contemporary culture, and in turn passed them on to later ages. Aspects of classical literature and thought appear throughout later literature and philosophy: for example, episodes from Roman history provide the material for plays by Shakespeare, operas by Verdi and novels by Robert Graves. Latin verse and prose styles have been imitated by countless authors, including Pope and Keats in English and Racine and Molière in French.

Index

Page numbers in italic denote map
references.

Further reading

J. Carcopino: *Daily Life in Ancient Rome* (translated by E. O. Lorimer, Penguin Books)

T. Cornell and J. Matthews: *Atlas of the Roman World* (Phaidon Books)

M. Grant and D. Pottinger: *Romans* (Thomas Nelson and Sons)

M. Hadas and others: *Imperial Rome* (Time-Life Books)

A. King: *Archaeology of Ancient Rome* (Bison Books)

Acknowledgment

The publishers wish to thank the Museo della Civiltà Romana, Rome,
for permission to base the reconstruction of Rome on pages 32-3 of this book
on their model of the ancient city.

First published in 1990 by Usborne Publishing Ltd,
83-85 Saffron Hill, London EC1N 8RT, England.

UE